Scripture Discussion Commentary 4

SCRIPTURE DISCUSSION COMMENTARY 4

Series editor: Laurence Bright

Prophets II

Ezekiel	*Francis McDonagh*
Minor prophets	*Hamish Swanston*
Daniel	*Bernard Robinson*

ACTA Foundation
Adult Catechetical Teaching Aids
Chicago, Illinois

First published 1972
ACTA Foundation (Adult Catechetical Teaching Aids),
4848 N. Clark Street, Chicago, Illinois 60640

Nihil obstat : John M. T. Barton STD LSS *Censor*
Imprimatur : + Victor Guazzelli *Vicar General*
Westminster, 3 July 1972

2541

Library of Congress number 71–173033
ISBN 0 87946 003 2
Made and printed in Great Britain by
William Clowes & Sons, Limited
London, Beccles and Colchester

Contents

v

Contents

General Introduction

A few of the individual units which make up this series of biblical commentaries have already proved their worth issued as separate booklets. Together with many others they are now grouped together in a set of twelve volumes covering almost all the books of the old and new testaments—a few have been omitted as unsuitable to the general purpose of the series.

That purpose is primarily to promote discussion. This is how these commentaries differ from the others that exist. They do not cover all that could be said about the biblical text, but concentrate on the features most likely to get lively conversation going—those, for instance, with special relevance for later developments of thought, or for life in the church and world of today. For this reason passages of narrative are punctuated by sets of questions designed to get a group talking, though the text of scripture, helped by the remarks of the commentator, should have already done just that.

For the text is what matters. Individuals getting ready for a meeting, the group itself as it meets, should always have the bible centrally present, and use the commentary only as a tool. The bibliographies will help those wishing to dig deeper.

What kinds of group can expect to work in this way?

Absolutely any. The bible has the reputation of being
difficult, and in some respects it is, but practice quickly
clears up a lot of initial obstacles. So parish groups of any
kind can and should be working on it. The groups needn't
necessarily already exist; it is enough to have a few like-
minded friends and to care sufficiently about finding out
what the bible means. Nor need they be very large; one
family could be quite enough. High schools (particularly
in the senior year), colleges and universities are also obvious places for groups to form. If possible they should
everywhere be ecumenical in composition: though all the
authors are Roman catholics, there is nothing sectarian
in their approach.

In each volume there are two to four or occasionally
more studies of related biblical books. Each one is self-
contained; it is neither necessary nor desirable to start at
the beginning and plough steadily through. Take up,
each time, what most interests you—there is very little in
scripture that is actually dull! Since the commentaries
are by different authors, you will discover differences of
outlook, in itself a matter of discussion. Above all, remember that getting the right general approach to reading the bible is more important than answering any
particular question about the text—and that this approach only comes with practice.

Volume four completes the commentary on the prophets: Ezekiel, who dominates the early period of the
exile, the ten who with Amos and Hosea (volume 2)
make up the 'minor prophets', and Daniel, the reflection
back from the Maccabean struggle into the heroic past.

L. B.

Ezekiel

Francis McDonagh

Introduction

Ezekiel is one of Israel's greatest theologians. It is largely due to him that the religion of Israel survived the exile in Babylon, and he is a representative of the unknown men who reworked the ancient traditions in exile to produce the bulk of the old testament as it exists today. It is difficult to appreciate the disaster which the collapse of Judah in 586 meant to believing Jews. It was the defeat of Yahweh (Jer 44:15ff), the death of the nation (Ez 37:11). One measure of its impact is the extent to which it drove Ezekiel to a reinterpretation of Israel's history, a passion which spills over into grotesque imagery (Ez 16; 23) and produced an unprecedented critique of salvation history (Ez 20:1-44). Another is the way it forced him into seeing Yahweh's action in a totally new way, the raising of Israel from the dead (Ez 37). Ezekiel took the old tradition of the exodus and reinterpreted it, but it was the idea of the holiness of God which enabled him to form a picture of the new covenant free from the limitations of the old. This notion of God's holiness seems at first sight utterly alien, so bound up is it with the ritual of the temple and its imagery (cf Ez 1; 22; 23). And yet this primitive idea was the catalyst which enabled Ezekiel to create images of God and his actions that were to be so

3

fruitful in the period of the new testament: the good shepherd (Ez 34), the new creation and the resurrection (Ez 36–37).

Modern biblical criticism, with its emphasis on the rootedness of the scriptures in their particular historical and cultural setting, warns us against making parallels between that world and our own, but nevertheless the example of Ezekiel, if not his every word, is relevant to an age which has heard of the death of God and is watching to see if a new christianity will emerge from the ruins of the old.

Book list

D. M. G. Stalker, *Ezekiel*, London 1968: a good, businesslike handbook to the text.

Walther Eichrodt, *Ezekiel*, a more complicated commentary by a famous German scholar on his own text of Ezekiel: speculative in both the good and bad senses.

G. von Rad, *Old Testament Theology*, 2 vols, Edinburgh and London 1962 and 1965.

1

Ezekiel's call
Ez 1:1–5:17

Ez 1:1–3. Introduction

These verses place Ezekiel in the first group of exiles (comprising the upper classes of the population) taken from Judah to Babylon with king Jehoiachin in 598 BC. His call will therefore have been, according to 1:2, in 594, and the latest date given in the book is 571 (29:17). The central event of Ezekiel's ministry, and the starting-point of his theology, was the fall of Jerusalem, which finally took place in 587. The whole of chapters 1–24 offer a justification and a theological interpretation of this event, and the extremes of language and action into which it drove Ezekiel show that it was also a personal crisis for the prophet himself.

The change from the first to the third person between 1:1 and 1:3 indicates the work of an editor, who has perhaps tried to explain the 'thirtieth year' of 1:1 and has given the book a formal title like those of the books of Haggai and Zechariah: 'the word of the Lord came'. This is the first of a set of fourteen dates in the book of Ezekiel (the others are at 3:16, 8:1; 20:1; 24:1; 26:1; 29:1, 17; 30:20; 31:1; 32:1, 17; 33:21; 40:1) which probably go back to Ezekiel himself or his immediate disciples. Like other prophetic books, the book of Ezekiel was worked over by later editors, and the original plan

5

seems to have been distorted to some extent. This is most
noticeable in the case of chapters 25–32, which have been
inserted as a section of oracles against the nations, breaking the connection between 24:27 and 33:21, and in
many other cases new material seems to have been added
to the original dated passages, so that the dates can be
safely taken to refer only to the material immediately
following them. The book in its present form falls into
four sections: 1–24, oracles against Jerusalem; 25–32,
oracles against the nations; 33–39, oracles of restoration;
40–48, the new Jerusalem and its temple.

The 'river Chebar' (1:3) has been identified as a tribu-
tary of the Euphrates now called Shatt-en-nil. It left the
Euphrates above Babylon, passed through Nippur and
rejoined the main river near Erech. The main group of
exiles were settled in the area south of Babylon, while
Jehoiachin and his household were kept in imprison-
ment in Babylon. The conditions of the exile do not seem
to have been particularly harsh; the Jewish community
kept its organisation, by means of the 'elders' (Ez 8:1;
14:1; 20:1), and there was communication between the
exiles and Jerusalem in the period before the city was
destroyed (see Jer 29). The main privation must have
been exile itself, and the main threat the disintegration of
the Jews as a distinct religious community. Particularly
in view of the centralising reforms of Josiah, the destruction of Jerusalem and its temple removed the focus of
Israel's religion. It had practically to be recreated, and
its survival and transformation into the system which
came to be known as judaism is due to the work of men
like Ezekiel, 'the father of judaism'. No doubt this feeling
of loss was strong only among a minority of the exiles,
but it could not fail to be the main pre-occupation of a
priest in the Jerusalem tradition, as Ezekiel was. The

strength of this feeling in Ezekiel explains why so much of his preaching to the exiles concentrates on Jerusalem, so much so that many commentators have suggested that he must have had two ministries, one in Jerusalem and a later one in Babylonia.

Ez 1:4–28. The vision of God

The strange symbolism of Ezekiel's vision makes it more rather than less difficult for a modern reader to feel the impact of what is being described, an impact which struck the prophet himself dumb for 'seven days' (3:15). The living creatures with their four faces and their wings, the fire and lightning and the whirling wheels with their rims full of eyes, are all combined to give an impression of what is ultimately indescribable, so that at the end of the overwhelming catalogue the prophet falls back on the bare statement: 'such was the appearance of the likeness of the glory of the Lord' (1:28). It is the presence of Yahweh himself, once thought of as visible only at the sacred centres of Israel's worship, the tabernacle or the most holy place in the temple (cf Ex 40:34; 1 Kg 8:11), but now appearing in an unclean land. The vision in itself is a powerful symbol of the shift in Israel's religious consciousness which the exile brought about in Ezekiel and, to a greater or lesser extent, in all believing Jews.

The text of this chapter has suffered from various expansions, which make it difficult to reconstruct the details of the original vision, but the details which are clear give an insight into the mental world to which Ezekiel belonged. As a priest, he had at his command the whole range of images used in the liturgy to describe the presence of Yahweh. The initial idea of a manifestation of God's presence is clearly presented in Ps 18:

> He bowed the heavens, and came down;
>> thick darkness was under his feet.
> He rode on a cherub and flew;
>> he came swiftly upon the wings of the wind (9–10)

The north, in Babylonian mythology, was the far-off dwelling place of the gods, and this idea is occasionally used in the old testament (Is 14:13; Ps 48:2). Thunder, fire and cloud are part of the manifestation of Yahweh on Sinai (Ex 19:16ff; 24:9ff). The living creatures, which are later (10:15) said to be cherubim, are obviously connected with the cherubim on top of the ark of the covenant, where, according to Ex 25:20ff, Yahweh would meet Israel. Cherubim were also part of the decoration of the inner sanctuary of Solomon's temple—see 1 Kg 6:23–28, where it is specifically mentioned that their wings touched. In the description of the 'firmament' (1:22) and the throne it is hard not to see a connection with the furnishings of the temple (see 1 Kg 6:23–28; 1 Kg 7:23–44): bronze is very important in both, and the 'bronze sea' in particular is generally regarded as being a representation of the 'firmament' (Gen 1:6) by which God tamed the primeval chaos. The rainbow (1:28) is the symbol of the covenant with Noah after the flood in the priestly theology (Gen 9:13–17).

The wheels (1:15–21) may be an addition to the original throne vision. They seem to add very little, and even to detract from the earlier statement that the living creatures derived their power from 'the spirit' (1:12), the spirit which sets Ezekiel on his feet again in 2:2 and brings the dry bones back to life (37:9–10). The wheels probably derive from the descriptions of the ark, which was transported on a cart (1 Sam 6:7ff).

The caution of 1:28 may reflect Ezekiel's theological training: note also 'the likeness of four living creatures' (1:5), 'the likeness of their faces' (1:10, 'the likeness as it were of a human form' (1:27). His reaction to the vision was, perhaps characteristically, expressed more expansively by Isaiah (6:5): 'Woe is me! For I am lost ... for my eyes have seen the King, the Lord of hosts!'

Ez 2:1–3:15. Ezekiel's commissioning

Ezekiel has bowed to the ground before the glory of Yahweh, the only proper attitude for a 'son of man'. This phrase means 'man', but with an emphasis on his weakness and limitations; this, at any rate, is the way it is used on the few occasions outside the book of Ezekiel that it appears in the old testament: '... man, who is a maggot, and the son of man, who is a worm' (Job 25:6; cf Ps 8:5). Ezekiel seems to have been the first to use it as a title, and it is probably from this that there developed its association with divine revelation, particularly in apocalyptic writings. In Daniel it is used both for the mysterious figure 'like a son of man' in the vision at 7:13 and as a title for Daniel himself at 8:17, and when Jesus uses it in the gospels he seems to be relying on an understood association with the last things.

Both ideas, the weakness of man in contrast to the power of God and selection by God for a special mission, are present in this passage, and we can perhaps feel Ezekiel's closeness to apocalyptic style, as later in the vision of the scroll (2:9–3:3). For such reasons Ezekiel has been called 'the father of apocalyptic', but his own book is on the whole very different from Daniel or Revelation.

We do not feel in Ezekiel, as in the two later books, that the whole action has to fit into a symbolic pattern. In Ezekiel the actions are still human and make sense, even if only in terms of an 'abnormal' personality. The only major exception to this is the final section of the book, with the vision of the temple and its measurements, where symbols seem to take over. Much of this section is later than the body of the book, but if some of it does go back to Ezekiel we may perhaps see it as one element (the 'priestly' as opposed to the 'prophetic'?) which in Ezekiel is kept in check by his obsession with Israel's relationship to Yahweh, but in the later authors has no such restraint. A useful comparison with Ez 1–3 is Rev 4–10, especially 4–5 and 10:8–11.

Another feature which sets Ezekiel apart from apocalyptic is the role of the 'spirit': 'And when he spoke to me, the Spirit entered into me and set me upon my feet' (2:2). As RSV's capital indicates, this must mean the spirit of Yahweh, the spirit which animates the living creatures. We have to make a conscious effort not to read into such passages a christian theology of the Spirit as a divine person, and one reason why it needs an effort is that Ezekiel's own theology moves in that direction. This is not the primitive formula of the early sagas, as in Jg 6:34 and 14:6 (Gideon and Samson), nor the theological statement of second Isaiah (Is 42:1, 61:1); there is a directness which makes one think of the Yahwist story of creation: 'the Lord God formed man of dust from the ground, and breathed into his nostrils the breath of life; and man became a living being' (Gen 2:7). This connection is made even stronger by the role of the spirit in bringing to life the dry bones in Ez 37. From another point of view, of course, this is Ezekiel's 'imagination', a fantasy, and there is no reason to deny that he could be

fitted into one of the categories of mental abnormality—
it would be more to the point to try and think of parallels
among modern theologians!

Ezekiel's commission has features in common with
those of both first Isaiah and Jeremiah (Is 6; Jer 1).
The idea that Israel is rebellious is a commonplace of
prophetic thought, and in Is 6:9–10 this is even said to
be brought about by Yahweh, but Ezekiel goes further in
suggesting that a foreign people would be readier to
listen. The experience of the exile forced Ezekiel to
make a complete reinterpretation of the idea of Israel as
the chosen people, and the result appears in chapter 20.
The scandalous idea that other nations might be pre-
ferred was taken up by Jesus (cf Mt 11:20–25). Like
Jeremiah, Ezekiel is warned against disappointment,
and he too has a pun in the account of his call: 'Like
adamant harder than flint . . .' is a pun on the prophet's
name, which in Hebrew means 'he makes hard' (cf
Jer 1:11–12). 3:11 makes explicit that Ezekiel's mission
is to the exiles.

3:16–27 seems to be misplaced. 3:16–21 is a summary
of chapters 18 and 33, perhaps placed here as part of the
definition of Ezekiel's ministry, and 3:22–27 seem to be
connected with chapter 4 and with 24:25ff and 33:21ff.

Ez 4:1–5:17. Prophetic actions

In this section and in 12:1–20 Ezekiel uses actions as
well as words to bring the message of Yahweh to his
people. Such symbolic acts were part of the prophetic
tradition of Israel. At first they are indistinguishable
from the stories of magic found in all legends—the stories
of Elijah and Elisha in the books of Kings are examples
of this—but gradually they are subordinated to the single

purpose of expressing the word of Yahweh. They become an extension of it, more than an illustration or a
device to attract attention, and symbolise God's power
in the life of his people. The fundamental meaning is
that, just as Yahweh intervenes so strikingly in the lives
of his prophets, so his power is directing the history of
Israel. Famous examples of such actions are Hosea's
marriage to a prostitute (Hos 1:3) and Isaiah's fathering
of a significantly named son at Yahweh's command
(Is 8:1–4). In Ezekiel's own time, Jeremiah had been
ordered not to marry (Jer 16) as a symbol of the extinc-
tion of the nation, but later is told to buy back a family
property as a sign of hope for the future (Jer 32).

    Ezekiel belongs to this tradition. His wife dies at the
time Jerusalem is under siege, and he is told not to
mourn for her, as a sign to the people that there will be
no ritual lament over the fall of Jerusalem (25:19ff,
esp 24, 27). But there is a new intensity about symbolic
activity in Ezekiel, a compulsiveness even about the
grubbing in the soil described in chapters 4–5 and 12,
and this seems to go with a stronger self-consciousness in
Ezekiel than in the earlier prophets about the importance
of these actions. It is repeatedly emphasised that these
are 'signs', or that he is a sign: 'I have made you a sign
for the house of Israel' (12:6), 'Ezekiel shall be to you a
sign; according to all that he has done you shall do'
(25:24; cf 4:3; 25:22, 27). Obviously, we have insuffi-
cient evidence to attempt a description of Ezekiel's personality, but the hints which come through his own description of his actions and visions are tantalising. He, of
course, is convinced of his mission and so were the disciples who preserved and edited his work, but it would
be a useful exercise to try to rewrite chapters 4–5 from
the point of view of an outsider. Our only hint of the

reaction of Ezekiel's own audience is in 33:30ff, which implies that he was one of the sights of Telabib.

Chapters 4–5 contain four symbolic actions. In 4:1–3 Ezekiel plays a war game. Mud brick was the normal material for writing on in Mesopotamia, and Ezekiel seems to have drawn a picture of a city on a brick and surrounded it with other objects to represent the siege. 'Even Jerusalem' (4:1) is a gloss; in the original version we are not told the name of the city until 5:5—it could have been Babylon!

4:4–17 is confused. It contains actions relating to the siege of Jerusalem and to the exile, but which is which is not always clear. Verses 7, 9b and 13 have been added to make clear links between their immediate context and either the siege or the exile, but not always correctly. The numbers in 4:4ff vary between the Hebrew manuscripts and the Septuagint, and this, together with the impossibility of carrying out the actions as described, have made some people regard it as a later addition. 4:10–11, 16–17 stand for the conditions of scarcity during a siege. 20 shekels is about 8 oz and a sixth of a hin is just under two pints.

4:12–15 concerns the uncleanness of food eaten in exile. For the uncleanness of human excrement see Deut 23:12ff. In exile it would be more difficult to observe all the dietary regulations, but even more we should probably think of the primitive idea of a foreign land being unclean in the sense of not dedicated to Yahweh: the exiles would be 'away from the presence of the Lord' (1 Sam 26:20). The pain of the exile was crystallised in the problems of worship (cf. Ps 137:4) and ritual meals, and it is striking that the thought of the latter provokes from Ezekiel one of the few protests we find in the book. His attitude recalls that of Peter in Acts (4:14; cf Ac 10:14).

In chapter 5 is the first of many violent threats against Jerusalem and its people. Ezekiel may be using the image of a razor which occurs in Is 7:20, but if so he has characteristically filled out the details of the earlier image. He has also developed it. The associations of shaving the head and beard in Hebrew thought are mourning and humiliation—it is a disfigurement—but in 5:1ff perhaps the most striking feature is the sword scattering the hairs. Themes occur in this chapter which are repeated through the first section of the book, the insistence on God's anger, provoked in particular by 'abominations' and rebellion against Yahweh's 'statutes and ordinances', and 'the nations'. As in 3:5–6, Israel is said to have been worse than the other nations. She was the centre of the nations (5:5), which is why her 'rebellion' was so terrible (5:6). Jerusalem was to be Israel's permanent dwelling-place and Yahweh's everlasting sanctuary (2 Sam 7:10ff), but it has been defiled (5:11). The glorious covenant with David, the whole basis of Yahweh's relationship with his people, is being destroyed. This is the message Ezekiel is forcing himself and his people to understand: 'I will do with you what I have never yet done, and the like of which I will never do again' (5:9).

1. *What are the various components of your image of God?*
2. *Are visionaries' descriptions of God likely to be less accurate than those of more sober theologians?*
3. *Was the exile really a disaster?*

2
The end
Ez 6:1–11:25

There is a clear structure in this section. After the general proclamation of destruction in chapters 4–5, chapter 6 condemns idolatry at country shrines, while chapter 7 intensifies this with its announcement of 'the end' for the 'land of Israel' and goes on to condemn 'violence' in the city. The climax is the vision of the destruction of Jerusalem and its temple in 8–11.

Ez 6:1–14. Against the mountains of Israel

This chapter contains at least three originally separate oracles, as can be seen from the repetition of the concluding formula: 'you/they shall know that I am the Lord' (6:7, 10, 13, 14). They have been put together here because of their common theme of destruction, and perhaps in particular because they contain the motif of the three agents of destruction, famine, sword and pestilence, which also appeared in chapter 5. 6:8–10 may be later than the other sections, as it seems to reflect the situation of the exiles rather than that of the inhabitants of the doomed city.

Why does Ezekiel address the mountains? He associates them with the 'high places', a technical term in the old testament for unorthodox sanctuaries, but to see them as no more than a symbol weakens the point. The defilement of the land is as fundamental a part of Ezekiel's message as the punishment of the people by exile. The promise of 'the land' was basic to Israel's relationship with Yahweh (see Ex 3), and its importance had been re-emphasised, about thirty years before Ezekiel began his ministry, by the Deuteronomic reform under king Josiah in 621. Josiah's reform, like the Davidic settlement four hundred years previously, had been both religious and political. Josiah had banned sacrifices anywhere except at the Jerusalem temple and had destroyed numerous other sanctuaries, including the ancient shrine of Bethel (cf 2 Kg 22–23, esp 23:8–9, 15–20). This was meant to promote a more uniform religious system throughout Judah, and the tone of the reform movement can be seen in the book of Deuteronomy, with its emphasis on 'the land' and worship only at 'the place which the Lord your God will choose' (Deut 12:5, 11, 14 etc). But religious unity was for Israel only the other side of political unity, and Josiah also tried to extend the power of the state. When he was defeated by Pharaoh Neco at Megiddo in 609, the religious as well as the political revival was discredited. On the one hand there was a relapse into the old tolerance of nature gods and foreign cults, from the feeling that the defeat of Josiah had proved the weakness of Yahweh (cf Jer 44:15–19). In men like Jeremiah and Ezekiel, however, the collapse of 609 provoked a complete reappraisal of the idea of a national religion. It made them see attempts to maintain the existence of Israel by political means as an obstacle to Yahweh's purposes and see in the power of Babylon his chosen instrument of punishment. The revolutionary nature of such an interpretation can be seen in Jeremiah's case from his hostile reception by his fellow-countrymen, and in the case of Ezekiel by the fury of his denunciation. The frequent condemnations of 'abominations' and the detailed descriptions of destruction and slaughter are to some extent stylised literary forms, but they also express the personal torment of a priest driven to attack the most holy things of his religion.

When Ezekiel attacks the mountains, he is attacking the physical backbone of the country, which included its political centres (Jerusalem, Samaria) and its most important holy places (Hebron, Jerusalem, Bethel, Shiloh, Shechem). Mountains in Hebrew thought were symbols of permanence and power, and here the mountains are the core of Israel, just as Mount Seir in chapter 35 represents the power of Edom. But mountains are also symbols of God's power, like the uncontrollable sea (Ps 36:5–6) and were traditionally associated with the worship both of Yahweh (Sinai, Mount Zion) and of the nature gods of the 'high places'.

Ezekiel sees 'dung-idols' (the Hebrew word he constantly uses, *gillulim*, is much stronger than merely 'idols') enthroned in Yahweh's place. In this he is in the main line of the prophets of Israel. From Elijah's legendary contest with the prophets of Baal (1 Kg 18) onwards, prophetic opposition testifies to the persistence of the cults of the 'high places', and by Jeremiah's time at least the term had become so formalised as to lose its association with actual hills (Jer 7:31). These cults were centred on the natural cycle of birth and rebirth, and were practised by the pre-Israelite inhabitants of Canaan as well as by the great powers of Mesopotamia with which Israel had to deal. Some involved sexual activity as sympathetic magic to promote fertility, while others worshipped personified aspects of the natural cycle, such as Tammuz (cf 8:14) or Baal, the god who descended to the underworld in the autumn and returned to life in the spring. The attraction of these cults in a pre-scientific agricultural society must have been strong, and from the point of view of the defenders of the pure worship of Yahweh their naturalness must have been their greatest threat; many people saw no reason why they should not combine them with the worship of Yahweh as a double assurance.

Ezekiel's attack on the high places emphasises the defilement which will take place. The presence of bodies or bones made a place ritually unclean and unusable for worship; this was Josiah's method of dealing with heterodox sanctuaries (2 Kg 23:15ff). In 6:9 'wanton' uses Hosea's traditional image of idolatry as sexual licence (Hos 4:12ff), which Ezekiel develops himself in chapters 16 and 23. 6:11ff is a paler version of chapter 21. The sword runs through the book of Ezekiel with a frightening randomness, and Ezekiel must have delivered such passages with no less frightening actions. 'From the wilderness to Riblah' (6:14) means from the southern to the northern borders of Judah. Riblah was the headquarters of Nebuchadrezzar in Syria to which Zedekiah was brought after his attempt to escape from the siege of Jerusalem in 586 (2 Kg 25:6).

Ez 7:1–27. The day of Yahweh

To bring the condemnation of Israel to a climax Ezekiel here uses two traditional prophetic concepts, the 'end' (cf Am 8:2ff) and the 'day of Yahweh' (cf Am 5:18–20; Is 2:12ff) and combines the two for greater effect. The 'day of Yahweh' was the day when Yahweh would destroy his enemies. In former times Israel saw it as the day when

Yahweh would lead their army to victory, but Amos had already stressed its ambiguity:

Woe to you who desire the day of the Lord!
  Why would you have the day of the Lord?
It is darkness and not light (Am 5:18)

Ezekiel achieves his effect by repetition and violence. It is a very different effect from the stateliness of Is 2:12ff, 'For the Lord of hosts has a day . . .' Ezekiel is beside himself: 'An end! The end has come . . . the end is upon you. . . . Behold, the day.' The normal course of things is disrupted, buying and selling, warfare, wealth: all are useless. The language of 7:14ff becomes even more violent and crude. 'Knees weak as water' (7:17) is a euphemism; the defenders are 'pissing themselves with fear.' 'An unclean thing' (7:19, 20) is the same word used to describe the ritual impurity of a woman's menstruation in 18:6; 22:10.

The worst thing of all is the capture by 'foreigners' of the holy land and the temple. They 'profane it' (7:21–22), not by introducing idols so much as by replacing the chosen people. It is the annulment of the covenant. Yahweh turns his face away (7:22; cf Num 6:25; Ps 109:24), ie he removes his presence. This, and the repeated emphasis, 'I will let loose my anger . . . I will judge . . . I will punish', stresses the enormity of what is happening. The vision in 8–11 will express this in another way, by describing the glory of Yahweh leaving the temple.

Ez 8:1–11:25. The temple vision

The date in 8:1 indicates the beginning of a new section, and the care with which the setting is described shows its importance. The leaders of the Jewish community are formally consulting Ezekiel. The elders were people of importance; they are among those addressed by Jeremiah in his letter in Jer 29. The beginning and end of the vision are also carefully noted (8:2; 11:24), not as a contrast with reality—a totally foreign idea in the context—but perhaps to emphasise the solemnity of the revelation.

Another reason for the careful note of the beginning and end of the vision is to mark off these four chapters as a single section. By its position here at the end of the oracles against the land, it is obviously meant to be the climax of judgement on Judah. The fact that it is a vision may also be significant here; Ezekiel is no longer announcing a judgement which is to come, foretelling what Yahweh will do, but seeing Yahweh at work. He no longer leaves it to his hearers to match his words against subsequent events, with all the possibilities of inaccuracy, but sees Yahweh at work in his own timelessness. For us the fact that we are presented with a vision, embellished with details like Ezekiel's being transported through the air by the hair of his head (8:3) and the description of the death of one of the baddies in mid-vision (11:13), makes us ask 'Is it real?' For Ezekiel, however, or at least for the final editors of his book, these qualities make it more rather than less real. This also explains why, in comparison, the historical fall of Jerusalem occupies such a minor place in the book (24:25–27; 33:21–22). In the present structure of the book the vision occurs six years before the fall of the city (8:1; 33:21), but it is the vision, not the messenger's words, which convince us that the city is lost, and tell us why. Having understood this fundamental fact, we can then take in its theological implications at leisure in the longer oracles which follow (chapters 12–24).

It is easy to see that the account of the vision as it stands has been put together out of independent units. Chapter 11 in particular seems to stand apart from the earlier version, and itself contains two separate units (11:1–13, 14–21). The references to the glory and the cherubim also seem to have been inserted rather awkwardly into the narrative of the vision (see especially 8:4; 9:3; 10:1, 3–5, 9–17). Some of them repeat, sometimes inaccurately, the description of the wheels and living creatures from chapter 1, and there is a suspicious anxiety to identify this vision with the previous one (8:4; 10:15, 20, 22).

The main point, at any rate, is clear even if the details are not. Ezekiel is shown foreign rites in the temple itself, at the entrance to the inner court (8:3) which surrounded the temple proper (the 'house'), in a room in the wall of the inner court (8:7–8) and finally in the inner court itself, in front of the entrance to the holy place (8:16). What exactly the 'image of jealousy' (8:3, 5) was is uncertain, but it is obviously a symbol of some cult. The 'creeping things and loathsome beasts' portrayed on the walls (8:10) may be part of an Egyptian cult, since the Egyptians rather than the Babylonians regarded certain animals as sacred—they are 'loathsome' because they are part of an alien cult. The 'seventy men of the elders of the house of Israel' are symbolic. Seventy elders were traditionally associated with Moses in his leadership of the people, and the formal description plays on that association (cf Ex 24:1, 9). The official representatives of the people have abandoned the worship of Yahweh. If this interpretation is correct, we should probably take the reference to 'Jaazaniah the son of Shaphan', as meaning the son of Shaphan the secretary, who was one of the leading figures in Josiah's religious reform (2 Kg 22:8–10);

if this is his son it is another sign of decline. Tammuz
(8:14) is the Babylonian equivalent of the vegetation god
known in Palestine as Baal, whose annual descent into
the underworld was celebrated by ritual mourning. In
some versions of the cult his sister Ishtar appeared as his
rescuer, and the weeping described here may be part of
the cult of the 'queen of heaven' mentioned in Jer 44:17ff.

The climax of the abominations is mentioned last.
It takes place at the focal point of Jewish ritual, where
the priests who went into the most holy place came out
and officiated in the sight of the people (cf Jl 2:17). This
space is now occupied by men who turn their back on the
house of the Lord, where his presence was enthroned,
and turn away to worship the sun, in accordance with
Mesopotamian practice. The seriousness of this is emphasised by Yahweh's exclamation, ending in the common refrain: 'my eye will not spare, nor will I have
pity' (8:17–18).

It is impossible to separate symbol from historical detail in the vision. Such details as the seventy elders and
the twenty-five men with their backs to the holy place
are obviously meant to emphasise the point that the
centre of the worship of Yahweh has been taken over by
other cults. On the other hand the account of Josiah's
reform in 2 Kg 23 (esp 23:5, 11–12) describes the worship of Baal, Asherah, the sun and planets as having been
carried on in the temple, and Jer 44 describes a controversy between Jeremiah and Jewish exiles in Egypt about
the worship of foreign gods. The attitude of the exiles is
parallel to that described here: 'The Lord does not see
us, the Lord has forsaken the land' (8:12; cf Jer 44:17–
18). The deportation of the king and the religious leaders,
especially coming so soon after the defeat of the orthodox
king Josiah, must have made many Jews lose faith in

their God; either he was so alienated from them that he would not listen to prayer, or he had been defeated by the gods of Egypt and Babylon. These events also affected Ezekiel, but in him one result was this description of Yahweh destroying his own sanctuary—an assertion of his continued power over events and also, paradoxically, of his continued interest in his people. Yahweh's direct involvement is emphasised in the text (esp 8:17–18; 9:4–8).

At the beginning of chapter 9 the tone changes to what we normally associate with apocalyptic writing. Crying with a loud voice seems to be a characteristic feature of this style (9:1; cf Rev 6:1; 10:3) and the seven supernatural agents of destruction have many successors in later Jewish writing, culminating in the new testament book of Revelation (cf esp Rev 4–11). To describe this turning point in the history of Israel Ezekiel seems to have drawn on both Babylonian and Jewish tradition. The number of the supernatural figures, seven, suggests associations with the seven planets known to the ancients, and in Babylonian mythology one of the planetary gods, Nebo, was 'lord of the pen'. The Babylonian gods also had their own characteristic weapons. In later Jewish writing there are said to be seven spirits or angels before God's throne (cf Tob 12:15; Rev 4:5), but this is the earliest occurrence of the idea, which may result from Jewish contact with Babylonian culture through the exile. The idea of a divine agent of destruction is familiar in Israel's tradition also. The most famous example is the killing of the first-born of the Egyptians at the exodus (Ex 12), and there, as here, those who were to be spared were given a special mark—though the mark here is more like the mark given to Cain (Gen 4:15). Such divine action was normally directed against the enemies of

God's people (cf 2 Kg 19:35), but an awareness gradually grew in Israel that their status as the people of God did not necessarily make them immune (cf 2 Sam 24:16). What is now taking place, however, is a much more radical breach between Israel and its God. Here Yahweh himself defiles his sanctuary, starting at its most holy place: ' "... begin at my sanctuary." So they began with the elders who were before the house. Then he said to them, "Defile the house ..." ' (9:6–7). The seriousness of the breach is re-emphasised by Yahweh's rejection of Ezekiel's appeal (9:8–10).

The action continues in 10:2, with the order to the man clothed in linen to take fire from between the cherubim and scatter it over the city. As fire taken from the presence of Yahweh, it would be doubly destructive. The idea behind this section seems to be that only a priest (linen clothing is priestly dress) could enter the holy of holies, and it is possible that the original account made the man in linen take fire from the most holy place in the temple (cf 10:2: 'Go in ... he went in'). At any rate the present text is hopelessly confused, and the description of the man scattering coals breaks off abruptly in the middle (10:8 'took it and went out'). Ignoring the description of the wheels and the cherubim, the movements of the glory are reasonably clear from 9:18–19 and 10: 22–23: from the holy place ('the house', 10:18) to the east gate, and from there to the mountain to the east of the city (the Mount of Olives).

11:1–25. The true Israel

The relationship between 11:1–14 and the earlier vision is hard to understand. There are points of connection: here as in 8:16ff there are twenty-five of the chief citizens ('princes of the people', 11:1; cf 'elders', 9:6) towards the east, but here they are apparently outside the temple, while the others were in the inner court. There is also a Jaazaniah in both accounts, though apparently not the same one. Perhaps originally the two stories were completely independent, and we may have here an example of the way the minds of the editors of Ezekiel's book worked when they put various pieces of text together.

Another difference between this section and chapter 8 is that Ezekiel's divine guide has now disappeared, and Ezekiel himself is more active. The details of the claim of the twenty-five are obscure, but the main point of the exchange seems to be the same as that of the oracle in 11:14–21—the survivors of destruction can gain no advantage by their own dishonest efforts, and the new Israel will be formed by God from the exiles by a completely new act of power (11:19). The later section has been inserted here to round off the vision section and balance the message of condemnation. It contains themes which are dealt with more fully in chapters 33, 34 and 36.

1. In industrialised countries religion is generally considered to be separate from politics. Is this

(*a*) *true in practice?*
(*b*) *a sign of progress or of the decline of religion—or*
(*c*) *does the one involve the other?*

2. Is there any event which would have a similar effect on christians today as the fall of Jerusalem had on Ezekiel?
3. Is religious exclusiveness justifiable?

3

Watchman over Israel
Ez 12:1–20:44

This section is central to an understanding of Ezekiel. It is as if he is working out the meaning of the experiences described in chapters 1–3 and 8–11. Chapters 12 and 13 tell us what he thought being a prophet meant; the principal task is supporting his people in their relationship with Yahweh, going up into the breaches, building a wall (13:5) or, as it is summed up in a later passage, being 'a watchman for the house of Israel' (33:7). What this means in practice can be seen in chapters 14 and 18. At the same time, Ezekiel's attempts to reinterpret the history of Israel produce some of the most powerful writing in the old testament (Ez 16; 19; 20), including a bitter criticism of salvation history which has no parallel in either the new or the old testament (20:1–44).

Ez 12:1–20. 'I am a sign for you'

In another symbolic action, Ezekiel mimes the situation of a deportee, forced to leave a captured city. He gathers together his essential belongings, and starts out in the evening, to avoid the hottest part of the day (12:4). This little drama is another example of Ezekiel's desperate anxiety to get through to a people who seemed impervious to his words (12:2). Note the repeated insistence on 'in their sight' (12:3, 4, 5, 6) and 12:11: 'I am a sign for you: as I have done, so shall it be done to them.' Ezekiel's whole life is taken over by his mission, to the extent of reducing him to trembling, unable to eat (12:18).

As with his diagram of a besieged city (4:1ff), it may not have been clear at first to Ezekiel's audience what he was doing; they may even have thought he was preparing for the end of exile. The explanation comes 'in the morning' (12:8). The text in its present form has been adapted to take account of the attempted escape of Zedekiah after the capture of Jerusalem (2 Kg 25:4; Jer 39:4; 52:7). His blinding by the Babylonians is alluded to in 11:13 ('I will bring him to Babylon . . . yet he shall not see it'), and the details of his escape have influenced the description of Ezekiel's mime (12:5–6; cf 12:12). To make the reference clear, an explanatory note has been added in 12:10.

Ezekiel's 'quaking' and 'trembling' (12:18) is almost certainly more than an act. It is impossible to separate his personality and his psychological condition from his prophetic ministry; it would be more accurate to say that it was through the disturbances in his personality that he became 'a sign' for the exiles. 12:19–20 probably exaggerates the desolation in Judah, certainly immediately after the fall of Jerusalem in 586, since Jer 39–40 describes an attempt to start something like normal life under Gedaliah, whom the Babylonians appointed 'governor of the cities' (Jer 40:5). For some people conditions may have improved, if only temporarily (cf Jer 39:10), and the harvest was good (Jer 40:12). These verses may therefore refer to conditions later, after Gedaliah's murder and the departure of many more

Jews to Egypt (Jer 42–43), or they may be a ritualised description of the fate of the rebellious city.

Ez 12:21–13:23. Prophecy

This section is very valuable for the information it gives us about Ezekiel's view of his activity as a prophet and also about the general situation of prophets in the society of Judah at this time. The effort to state his position forces him to unusual eloquence and reveals a tenderness behind the violence of his condemnation (13:18–19; cf 14:5).

The problem of distinguishing between true and false prophets existed in Israel from the beginning of the prophetic movement. In a sense, it may have been an essential feature of the movement that there should be dispute between its members, and the disputes tended to centre on the relations of the prophets to the monarchy. The monarchy was a centralising force in religious as in political matters, inevitably since the pre-Hebrew kings of the Canaanite city-states had religious functions and the Hebrew monarchy was based on the Canaanite pattern. The innovation provoked opposition among the Hebrews, and the hostile account of the institution of the monarchy in 1 Samuel attributes it to the Hebrews' desire to be 'like the nations' (1 Sam 8; esp 8:4; cf the earlier and more favourable account of the new institution in 1 Sam 9:1–10:16). The canonical prophets may even have belonged to a religious group which tried to preserve a purer idea of Yahweh's kingship against the encroachments of the monarchy. The kings of Israel and Judah probably kept prophets as paid seers as did the kings of Assyria and Babylon, but the great prophets are always presented in the old testament as distinct from such court prophets, and often in opposition to them. Conflict between the two sorts of prophet is an important theme in the books of Kings, and the distinction between them was complicated because both groups spoke in the name of Yahweh (cf 1 Kg 22, esp 22:11–12, 24).

Another reason for the difficulty in distinguishing between true and false prophets is that they often claimed to speak in Yahweh's name in areas where the connection between his will and actions was harder to see. This is particularly true of political matters. It is easy for us, looking back, to say that Israel's religious heritage was preserved by the work of men like Jeremiah and Ezekiel, but at the time things were much less clear. Not only were Jeremiah and Ezekiel defeatist in military affairs, and thus lowered morale at a time of national crisis, but they also invoked the authority of Yahweh for blasphemous attacks on religious institutions—in spite of his promise that he would not allow his holy city to be destroyed.

The death of king Josiah was the beginning of the final crisis of the Hebrew monarchy, and a time of unprecedented political and religious confusion. Jeremiah's ministry covered the whole period from the Deuteronomic reform (621) to the destruction of Jerusalem (586), and the book of Jeremiah has frequent references to false prophets (cf esp Jer 27–29). Jeremiah also gives us the names of two rivals of Ezekiel's in Babylon, Ahab the son of Kolaiah and Zedekiah the son of Maaseiah (Jer 29:15–21). The issue between Ezekiel and such men was the same as that between Jeremiah and his rivals: would Yahweh really go back on his promises and abandon Jerusalem? Jeremiah and Ezekiel, in both cases only after an inward struggle, had come to the conclusion that it was Yahweh's will that Jerusalem, the temple and the whole existing institution of Israel's religion should be destroyed. This conviction became the basis of their preaching, so much so that Jeremiah could even say that the only true prophecies were bad ones (Jer 25:5–9). It is possible that Jeremiah and Ezekiel knew each other though neither mentions the other, but certainly each must have known the other's work, through messages between Babylonia and Jerusalem (cf Jer 29) if not more directly. One strong piece of evidence for contact is in Ez 13, where Ezekiel apparently uses a saying of Jeremiah as the basis for an attack on false prophets (Ez 13:8–16; cf Jer 6:14; 8:11). False prophets bolster the people's hopes but their words have no substance: they are a wall finished with whitewash but with no mortar ('daub') underneath.

Optimism, then, at this period was one sign of false prophecy: the prophets of comfort have not been sent by Yahweh (Ez 13:6) but 'prophesy out of their own mouths' and 'follow their own spirit' (13:2, 3). But seeing things this way meant first accepting the message of Jeremiah and Ezekiel, and both of these tried to find other criteria which would convince the uncertain. The difficulty of the problem is shown by Jeremiah's tortuous attempt to deal with it (Jer 23:9–32). He attacks the morals of the false prophets (23:14) and their use of dreams (23:25–28), but finally falls back on the claim that the word of Yahweh itself shows its superiority: 'What has straw in common with wheat? says the Lord. Is not my word like fire, says the Lord, and like a hammer which breaks rocks in pieces?' (Jer 23:28–29).

For Ezekiel, the main criterion is the true prophet's concern for his people's relationship to Yahweh. It is this which he works to repair, to defend the people against the anger of their God (13:5). There is an unexpected note of compassion in this section, which reappears in Ezekiel's condemnation of the women magicians (13:17–23). As much as the infringement of Yahweh's rights over life and death, it is the despair in Yahweh's mercy they create which provokes his anger (13:20–22). In this we see Ezekiel carrying out his pastoral mission among the people, which is a new feature in prophecy and no doubt created in part to meet the situation of the exile. Ezekiel's view of his mission is elaborated in chapter 33. Again in chapter 14, Ezekiel insists that true prophecy is incompatible with idolatry, which estranges the people from Yahweh (14:4–5).

Two of the abuses of prophecy which Ezekiel condemns might be expected to be obvious, magic and association with idolatry, but the problem of discerning God's will in the life of his people, which was the central problem of Ezekiel's mission, was much more difficult when all the old securities had been swept away. Jeremiah suggested that God's word spoke for itself (Jer 23:28–29), but probably neither he nor Ezekiel thought of understanding it as a simple process. We will almost certainly be wrong if we imagine Ezekiel as having the answers ready, and should probably see the allegories in chapters 16, 20 and 23 as an attempt to find answers, to reinterpret the history of Israel in order to make sense of its present. The interpretation depends on faith, but this does not exclude a critical approach—we must not underestimate the effort it cost Ezekiel to oppose the orthodoxy of his day. A religion which believes in a God acting in history will always have to face prophecy. It was true of Israel, it was true of the first christian community, and it is no less true of the churches today. In no case is the truth easy to reach: many, even the elect, may be led astray (cf Mt 24:11, 24; Eichrodt is interesting on the problem of prophecy in the new testament; see his *Commentary*, 175–178).

Ez 14:1–23. Judgement on Israel

If we can speak of Ezekiel developing the traditional pro-phetic ministry in the new direction of pastoral care, in this chapter we see the pastoral ministry in action. Obviously it answered the new conditions of exile, in which the regular temple liturgy was impossible and religious organisation at local level may have been dis-rupted. But this was not something anyone could take up. Given the confusion and demoralisation among priests and prophets we read about in Jeremiah and Ezekiel (even making allowances for the exaggeration of pole-mic), it must have taken the clear line of an Ezekiel to win any response at all from the exiles—the scepticism Ezekiel answered in 12:21ff must have been reinforced by exile. Nor can it have been pleasant hearing for the elders who did come to such a consultation as this. And yet the word 'pastoral' is appropriate in view of the ur-gency with which the prophet insists on Yahweh's desire to repair his people's relationship with him, 'that I may lay hold of the hearts of the house of Israel' (14:5). The language is violent, but it is nonetheless the language of love, the violent love described in the allegories of chapters 16, 20 and 23, which is a valuable corrective to any comfortable ideas about God. The ultimate aim is the restoration of the covenant relationship expressed in the cultic formula, 'that they may be my people and I may be their God' (14:11), but in a new and purified form, with a new understanding of God's justice and holiness (14:23).

The urgency and violence of Yahweh's desire can be

seen in the fact that he answers the elders' inquiry himself (14:4, 7) in spite of their idolatry. In giving the answer Ezekiel uses the style of the priestly law known as 'casuistic' because of its attempt to cover all cases: 'any one of the house of Israel, or of the strangers that sojourn in Israel, who . . . and yet . . .' (14:7; cf Lev 17; 22). This style continues in the next section, 14:12–20, with various aspects of the judgement analysed separately: 'When a land . . . even if . . . If . . ., even if . . . Or if . . .' The effect of this is to make the pronouncement more solemn, to raise a particular condemnation to the status of a general law. This applies more particularly to the first section (14:6–11), which retains the legal form and ends with a judgement formula (14:10), but in the second Ezekiel makes use of this form to emphasise the seriousness of the punishment. He is not in fact here examining different cases as in 18:5ff, but simply bringing out different aspects of a single event, and finally he abandons the pretence of reasoning altogether and contradicts himself in 14:22: 'Yet there will be survivors . . .' (RSV's conditional is wrong).

Noah, Daniel and Job are three traditional types of righteousness taken from non-Hebrew culture. In a similar saying, Jeremiah uses examples from the tradition of Israel, Moses and Samuel (Jer 15:1–4). The idea behind the passage is the same as that in Abraham's plea for Sodom in Gen 18:22–33, but the bargain is no longer acceptable. Jerusalem will suffer even more than the hypothetical faithless land (14:21), and the survivors are not saved for their own sake but to be a vindication of God's righteousness. This is a rather bleak consolation, and the introduction of that idea in 14:22b, 23a may be a later addition.

Ez 15:1–8. Useless vinewood

The vine was one of the most valued products of Israel, and appears as one of the attractions of the land flowing with milk and honey in Num 13:23. It also soon became a literary symbol for the people of Israel, as in Ps 80:8ff: 'Thou didst bring a vine out of Egypt . . .' The prophets took it up, and developed it into a symbol of Israel's infidelity. Isaiah's famous song, 'My beloved had a vineyard on a very fertile hill' (5:1–7) describes how in spite of Yahweh's care the vine yielded wild grapes, and Jeremiah uses the same idea (Jer 2:21). In contrast, the vine branch in this passage of Ezekiel has no fruit at all. It is bare wood, and of poor quality, no good for making anything. Furthermore it is burnt at both ends and the middle is charred. The splendour has vanished. Israel has been wiped out, the leaders of Judah have been deported and Jerusalem has only a little time left before it is destroyed by fire.

Ez 16:1–43. Israel's insatiable lust

Again in this, one of his most powerful passages, Ezekiel takes an existing symbol for Israel and presses it to its limits, almost, one might say, degrades it. The idea of Israel as Yahweh's bride comes from Hosea, and a comparison of this chapter with Hos 2:2ff will show what Ezekiel has done to it. The simple beauty and pathos of Hosea's poem are replaced in Ezekiel by overwhelming disgust and indignation. Details are piled up to produce a meticulous description of depravity. This awkwardness has led many commentators to argue that an original allegory of Ezekiel's has been expanded, since there is an obvious expansion in the last part of the chapter (16:43b–63). On the other hand, there are no clear signs to show what the original text was, and it is a testimony to the skill of the later editors, if there were any, that the commentators disagree about whether the alleged expansions are by Ezekiel himself or disciples. The full power of Ezekiel's work can only be seen if we realise that its aim and effect is different from Hosea's and admit that its power depends on the obsessive association of blood, sex and worship.

Ezekiel's allegory describes the history of Yahweh's relationship with Israel, and from the start Ezekiel is at pains to exclude any basis for pride. He insists on Israel's identity with the very nations she had made such efforts to disassociate herself from, the pre-Hebrew inhabitants of Palestine (Canaanites or Amorites). There is historical truth in this, since Jerusalem did not come under Hebrew control until the time of David (cf 2 Sam 5:6–10), and there is some evidence for Hittite connections with the city in the remoter past. Ezekiel's main point, however, is to cut out the patriarchs completely and so to remove any grounds for boasting of the merits of these friends of God. In this scheme of things there is no room for any claim to be 'children of Abraham' (cf Mt 3:9; Jn 8:39).

The point, of course, is that Israel's election depends totally on Yahweh, and this is reinforced in the story of the abandoned baby girl. Israel depends on her God for her very life ('And . . . I said to you . . . "Live"', 16:7), and even then she is naked until her lover gives her clothes. The story follows the fairy-tale pattern of the prince who falls in love with a poor girl, but Ezekiel has ruthlessly excluded any note of sentiment or magic. Instead we have a neutral, detailed account both of the missing post-natal care of the new-born child and of Hebrew courtship and marriage practices. The allegory goes on to trace the history of Israel, through the covenant

at Sinai (16:8) to the grandeur of the monarchy
(16:12ff), and the tension of the comparison is skilfully
held by the use of images which apply equally to the or-
phan girl become a royal bride, to Israel in its covenant
with Yahweh and to the style of the monarchy. There
may even be implied references to the temple worship
('my oil and my incense', 16:18). The imagery continues
in the description of religious infidelity; as a prostitute
dresses and makes up, so Israel decorated the shrines of
other gods. Indignation breaks with the reference to
passing children through fire and we come back to the
basic relationship—'Were they not my children?' says
Yahweh.

Religious infidelity leads into political disloyalty and
alliances with Egypt, Assyria and Babylon. There is a
connection between religious and political matters here
at two levels. First, historically, political relations with
another state, especially a more powerful one, involved
some degree of recognition of their gods. Even apart
from this technical idolatry, however, alliances in themselves were regarded by the prophetic tradition as an
abandonment by Israel of her position as a people whose
loyalty was due to Yahweh alone. Ezekiel's disgust intensifies now: Israel is worse than a prostitute, who sells
her body for gain, she is that phenomenon which terrified
male-dominated ancient societies, a women who actively
seeks her own satisfaction (cf the *Agamemnon* of Aeschy-
lus). The punishment Ezekiel decrees is a mixture of the
traditional penalties in Israelite law for adultery, strip-
ping and stoning (16:38:40; cf Lev 20:10), to which
Ezekiel adds dismemberment, and the actual fate of
Israel and Judah, invasion and destruction (16:37, 38,
41). After all this, incredibly to our way of thinking,
Yahweh becomes calm; his justice is satisfied (16:42-43).

Ez 16:43b–58. Jerusalem, Samaria and Sodom

This is an addition to the original story. In this bald allegory, with little life and direct equivalence between the terms of the comparison, the setting of the first story has been changed. The abandoned girl now has her own sisters. The reference has changed too; Jerusalem is now the daughter of a wicked mother, perhaps a daughter of the Israel described in the first story. An interesting feature is that in this passage Sodom's sin is described as pride, not sexual perversion as in Genesis 18, which may be evidence of a different tradition. This passage itself seems to have suffered alteration, with the original version making Jerusalem lower than Samaria and Sodom (16:47–48, 51–52, 57–58; cf the updated version in the new testament, Mt 11:20–24), and softened by the addition of a promise of equal restoration (16:53–55).

Ez 16:59–63. Restoration

This section seems to be a composite to draw both the previous allegories together. 16:59–60 refers to the covenant and 'the days of your youth' (16:8, 43), while 16:61 refers to the sisters of the second allegory. The phrases 'establish' and 'everlasting covenant' are characteristic of the Priestly strand in the Pentateuch, and for this reason it has been suggested that they are later than Ezekiel, who talks at 34:25 and 37:26 of 'a covenant of peace'.

Ez 17:1–24. A political allegory

The allegory this time is a nature fable. Its subject, as the commentary in 17:11–21 shows, is the policies of Zedekiah, whom Nebuchadrezzar had substituted for

Jehoiachin on the throne of Judah. For a fuller account of
these events see 1 Kg 24:8–25:7; Jer 37:5ff. It is quite
likely that this was a commentary on contemporary events,
since the reference to the fate of Zedekiah in 17:19ff is
sufficiently vague (cf 12:10ff) not to be hindsight, and
Ezekiel was quite convinced, without needing any further
evidence, that attempts to resist Babylon were against
Yahweh's will and would lead to disaster (cf Jer 27:1ff).

The imagery Ezekiel uses is traditional. Jeremiah refers to Nebuchadrezzar as an eagle (Jer 48:40; 49:22),
and in Babylonian art an eagle was the symbol of the sun-
god. The cedar is associated in the old testament particularly with the grandeur of the Davidic monarchy
(Solomon's use of cedar in his building obviously impressed the author of the book of Kings), while Zedekiah,
not being the legitimate king, is merely 'the seed of the
land' (17:5). It seems to be characteristic of Ezekiel's
style to press every detail of his images. Here the 'top-
most of its young twigs' stands for the young Jehoiachin
and the leading citizens, and the way the vine grows
represents the limitations of Zedekiah's political freedom
and his dependence on Babylon. The second eagle is
Egypt, to which Zedekiah appealed for help against
Babylon (cf Jer 37:5ff), and 'he' and 'the east wind'
(16:9, 10) are the avenging Nebuchadrezzar.

Both Jeremiah and Ezekiel regarded attempts to
escape from the power of Babylon as disobedience to
Yahweh, but Ezekiel sees Yahweh's influence as much
more direct. Zedekiah's vassal treaty with Babylon is
equated with an oath and covenant to Yahweh (16:19).
This is comparable with the view Ezekiel takes elsewhere:
in 14:9 Yahweh deceives the prophet who answers the
idolaters, and in 20:25 Yahweh is responsible for making
Israel sacrifice their children to Moloch. So far is Ezekiel

driven in his attempts to assert the power of Israel's god in the face of his apparent utter collapse before the Babylonian invader.

The last section of the chapter, 17:22–24, contrasts human attempts to build national power with the work of Yahweh. The type of power here is also different. Israel's glory in the new age will not come from the domination of other nations but will be a symbol of Yahweh's lordship for other nations to see (the beasts, birds and trees, 16:23–24). The imagery of the cedar is used in this way by Ezekiel later to describe Egypt, and a similar image appears in Dan 4, cf esp 4:10–12, 20–22. Similar pictures of the exaltation of Jerusalem can be found in Is 2:2–4 ('It shall come to pass in the latter days that the mountain of the house of the Lord shall be established as the highest of the mountains . . .') and in the post-exilic Is 60 ('nations shall come to your light, and kings to the brightness of your rising'), but the present one is much more restrained: the nations shall know the power of Yahweh (17:24).

Ez 18:1–32. An offer of life

On a first reading this chapter may seem to be no more than the assertion of a mechanical view of divine justice, hardly justifying the rhetorical question in 18:23. Taken in context, however, it turns out to have almost precisely the opposite message.

The key to the interpretation is in 18:2 and 18:25. It is a polemic against an attitude Ezekiel has argued against before, the despair which may be either cynical as in 12:21–28 or resigned as in 37:11. The saying about the sour grapes is also quoted in Jer 31:29, which supports the statement that it was a current saying. A similar saying occurs in Lam 5:7: 'Our fathers sinned and are no more; and we bear their iniquities.' In other words, it is an excuse, an attempt by the generation of the exile to transfer the blame for the present disaster on to their ancestors. This is one reason for the severe tone.

The form of 18:5ff, 10ff, 14ff, with its enumeration of cases followed by a formal judgement, 'he is righteous' or 'He shall not live,' is based on a liturgical form, possibly on a ritual examination made by the priest of worshippers coming to the temple (cf Pss 15, 24), and the offences listed are those which cut a man off from membership of the religious community. In this aspect, relationship with God is almost mechanical: his holiness is such that it is incompatible with certain forms of behaviour, and this is why Ezekiel can say of the righteous man who falls, 'None of the righteous deeds which he had done shall be remembered' (18:24). On the other hand, Ezekiel severely circumscribes the field of the inevitable; in the life of each generation and of each individual there is a possibility of repentance. In this sense Ezekiel is qualifying the harshness of Israel's primitive theology as seen in Ex 20:5: 'I the Lord your God am a jealous God, visiting the iniquity of the fathers upon the children to the third and the fourth generation of those who hate me,' though others had done this before him. 2 Kg 14:6 ascribes to 'the book of the law of Moses' the rule that 'the fathers shall not be put to death for the children, or the children for the fathers; but every man shall die for his own sin'.

Ezekiel 18 is sometimes described as an assertion of individual responsibility against old ideas of corporate guilt, but this is only part of the truth. Ezekiel insists on individual punishment in the strictest terms, but this is not in opposition to the idea of a national destiny. The idea of a special election of Israel lies behind all Ezekiel's work, all his energies were devoted to working out and describing to his people the new form this could take when the old was shattered. The idea of Yahweh's dealing with Israel as a whole was the premise of the allegory of chapter 16, as it is again of chapters 20 and 23, and in this chapter itself, at 18:25 and 18:30, appeal and judgement are addressed to 'the house of Israel'. What Ezekiel is attacking is a misrepresentation of the idea of Israel's solidarity born of despair, and his first step is to break through the complacency expressed in the opening proverb. Having brought the exiles to face their true situation, he can then show them Yahweh's underlying motive in what one commentator describes as 'one of the most evangelical utterances of the Old Testament—Have I any pleasure in the death of the wicked, says the Lord, and not rather that he should turn from his way and live?' (18:23). Judgement can then turn into an offer of life which looks forward to the restoration oracles in chapters 34, 36 and 37.

Ez 19:1–14. A lamentation for the kings of Judah

This chapter is a poem in the traditional Hebrew form of a *qinah* or death lament. In view of the abrupt opening it may originally have followed chapter 17, which is also a poem in the original. The lion was a traditional royal symbol in Judah, and has been found on a seal at Megiddo; cf Gen 49:9: 'Judah is a lion's whelp.' The first section is about Jehoahaz, the successor to Josiah chosen by the people but deposed by Pharaoh Neco and taken to Egypt (2 Kg 23:30–34), and either Jehoiachin or Zedekiah, both of whom were taken to Babylon. 19:10–14 widens the view to the Davidic dynasty as a

whole, now symbolised by the vine. 19:11 refers to the
kings of Judah, the 'branches' (plural, not 'stem' as in
RSV), and the fate of the vine is the same as that described
in chapter 17. This dignified and moving poem shows the
falsity of the common view of Ezekiel as an implacable
judge welcoming Judah's tragedy.

Ez 20:1–44. Israel's history of sin

This is one of the most important chapters in the book.
It is the second of the three great surveys of Israel's
history—the others are in chapters 16 and 23—and the
one in which Ezekiel makes his most detailed effort to
understand how the history of the people chosen by
Yahweh could have ended in such apparent failure.
Ezekiel's interpretation of Israel's history here is unique
in the old testament, and even verges on blasphemy
when he claims that Yahweh deliberately gave Israel the
commandment to sacrifice their first-born.

The importance of the chapter is underlined by the
giving of a date; this is another solemn address to the
people like the one in chapter 14, and the same formal
title is used again here: 'elders of Israel'. The subject on
which the elders wanted advice is not clear, but from
20:31–32 it seems as if it had to do with worshipping
Yahweh in a foreign land. It has even been argued that
they had a plan to establish a system of sacrifices in
Babylon (see Eichrodt, 273ff). Whatever their hopes,
they are rejected, and Ezekiel is told instead to judge
them (20:4). He does this through a summary of Israel's
history in the wilderness. Unlike the historical surveys in
Ez 16 and 23, this summary almost completely ignores
the history of the monarchy; the only mention of entry
into the promised land is in 20:27–29, which may be a

later insertion. The reason for this can perhaps be seen from a comparison with Deuteronomy. Deuteronomy, which was the centrepiece of Josiah's reform in 621, is an extended sermon to the people of the late seventh century in the form of a final address by Moses to Israel in the wilderness immediately before the entry into the promised land. Deuteronomy tried to impose on the corrupt seventh century the pure ideal of Israel encamped in the wilderness under the direct guidance of Yahweh and his servant Moses (cf Deut 1:1; 4:1; 5:1; 6:1; 12:1). Ezekiel also emphasises the wilderness (20:10, 13, 21, 23) and the promise of the good land (20:6, 15). He uses the Deuteronomic phrase 'statutes and ordinances' (20:11, 13, 16, 19, 21, 24; cf Deut 4:1, 5, 8, 14) and the 'name' of God in a similar way to stand for his presence with Israel (20:9, 14, 22; cf Deut 12:5, 11 etc), and the prominence given to the charge of idolatry is also Deuteronomic (20:7-8, 16, 18, 24, 26, 21; cf Deut 4:15ff; 7:4ff; 9:12ff; and cf esp Ez 20:32 and Deut 4:28). It looks as if Ezekiel, like the authors of Deuteronomy, is taking the Israel of the exodus as the norm, the model from which her true relationship to Yahweh can be seen. In the second half of the chapter (20:32-44) the Babylonian exile is presented as a new exodus (20:34-36), with the difference that the power which was first used against Egypt (the 'mighty hand and outstretched arm', 20:34, another Deuteronomic phrase, cf Deut 4:34; 7:19) now turns into judgement on Israel.

Ezekiel may share with Deuteronomy the idea that the people of the exodus are the model for Israel's relationship with Yahweh, but his assessment is very different. Deuteronomy emphasises the lack of faith of the exodus community, which Yahweh punished by preventing Moses and the 'evil generation' from entering the promised land (cf Deut 1:19–40), but its dominant conviction is one of security in the protection of Yahweh. The national renewal initiated by Deuteronomy would win back Yahweh's favour and make Israel great again; in fact one of the motives for renewal is pride in the greatness of Yahweh and his deliverance of Israel (cf Deut 4:32–40). Deuteronomy itself is careful to separate this from any greatness attaching to Israel herself (cf Deut 7:7–8), but this awareness must have been lost in the zeal for national reconstruction under Josiah—at least so it seems if we are to judge from the collapse of morale which followed Josiah's death. Ezekiel, on the other hand, will allow no room for pride in God's act of deliverance, and in this he takes a blacker view even than Jeremiah who, in spite of his rejection of Israel's religious institutions, can look back to the exodus as Israel's honeymoon with Yahweh:

> 'I remember the devotion of your youth,
>   your love as a bride,
> how you followed me in the wilderness,
>   in a land not sown.
> Israel was holy to the Lord . . . (Jer 2:2–3)

Ezekiel, even harder here than in chapter 16, has simply turned the history of salvation into a history of sin (cf 'the abominations of their fathers'). The earlier traditions know of reluctance and rebellion on the part of Israel in Egypt (Ex 5:19–6:9) and later (Ex 14:11–14; 32:15ff; Num 11; 14:1–11), but Ezekiel accuses Israel of idolatry even in Egypt. There is no hint of this in the earlier accounts, which Ezekiel obviously knows (Ez 20:5–7; cf Ex 20:2; Deut 25:9). This makes it clear that Ezekiel is not merely repeating existing traditions, but using them to create something totally new, a judgement (20:4).

The most striking part of this interpretation is in 20:25–26, where Ezekiel makes Yahweh claim that he 'gave them statutes which were not good and ordinances by which they could not have life'. This is blasphemy. It is much more than the claim that Yahweh deceives false prophets (1 Kg 22:22); Ezekiel here presents Yahweh as deliberately poisoning the source of Israel's life, the law (cf 20:11, 13, 21). The commandment he means is Ex 34:19, 'All that opens the womb is mine', which requires the sacrifice (Ex 13:2, 15) of the firstborn of all animals. In the case of children this regulation is commuted by the Pentateuch—firstborn children are not to be sacrificed, but 'redeemed' by the substitution of an animal (Ex 34:20; 13:13)—and it seems clear that in the historical period child sacrifice was not regarded as part of the worship of Yahweh but, on the contrary, as a Canaanite perversion (cf Deut 12:31; 2 Kg 16:3; 21:6). Here again, Ezekiel rejects the tradition and ascribes this abomination to the law given in the wilderness, before Israel could have been influenced by her neighbours in Palestine.

It is possible that Ezekiel knows of more cases of child sacrifice in Israel than are recorded in the old testament, although archaeological evidence seems to support the tradition. There is also some evidence that child sacrifice took place as part of the religious confusion of the late seventh century (cf Jer 7:31; 19:5; 32:35), but Ezekiel's reaction is still indefensible. What Jeremiah solemnly denounces, he ascribes to Yahweh's sadism ('that I might horrify them', 20:26). This statement cannot be explained away, nor can it be justified as an assertion of Yahweh's power over events, both good and evil. The famous new testament description of God's wrath in Rom 1:18ff is not parallel, because in Romans God gives

men up to their own vices. Ezekiel's attitude here is the
same as that in Ez 14:9, where Yahweh says he 'deceives'
a prophet who gives an answer to idolaters. It would be
possible to understand that passage as meaning that idolaters inevitably receive the word of Yahweh in a distorted
form because of their prior dispositions (though that is
not what Ezekiel says), but the present passage does not
invite such treatment. The God of Ez 20:25–26 is
different from the stern judge of Ez 18 and the vengeful
husband of Ez 16, and, more strikingly, from the God
who restores Israel in 20:32–44. In all other descriptions
of God's anger some form of justice comes in, however
ruthless it may seem. Is the answer that the only possible
explanation for this statement lies in Ezekiel's psychology?
There seems no reason to deny that the form of Ezekiel's
message was determined by disturbances of his personality, possibly produced by the experience of the fall of
Jerusalem and exile, and it has been suggested that
Ezekiel was a schizophrenic. Attaching such a term to
Ezekiel is extremely speculative, since not only is our
evidence slight but the category itself is also not clearly
defined. We are on firmer ground, however, when we
move from the prophet to his book and it is not too much
to say that there could be no more striking or more important example of schizophrenia in the book of Ezekiel
than his God.

The second half of this section, 20:32–44, is sufficiently
different in tone from the first for many commentators
to have suggested that it was written later, after the fall
of Jerusalem. Even if this is so, it has been carefully
constructed to form a conclusion to the first section.
The wilderness of Egypt is now 'the wilderness of the
peoples' (20:35), the scene of judgement on Israel after
a new exodus ('I will bring you out', 20:34). Only now

(if 20:27–29 are an addition) does Israel enter the land. The description of the restored people is in religious terms. They serve Yahweh on his holy mountain, with acceptable offerings ('contributions' and 'gifts', 20:40, are technical terms of the liturgy) instead of their former idolatry. The final verse emphasises that this is not due to any merit of theirs, but for the glory of Yahweh ('for my name's sake', 20:44; cf 20:41: 'I will manifest my holiness').

(For a different interpretation of this section, and in particular of its relation to Deuteronomy, see Eichrodt's *Commentary*, esp 272–76.)

1. Can you think of any modern prophets? Would you include non-christians? Give reasons.

2. Leading christians today give totally opposed assessments of the state of christianity (and of most other things!). Can they be divided into true and false prophets?

3. Should the name 'prophet' be reserved to people who have something to say about world issues rather than purely religious ones? On which side of the line would Ezekiel stand?

4. Can the God of Ezekiel 20:25 form part of our picture of God, or should it be dismissed as an aberration? If we include it, what difference does it make?

5. Can christian history be reinterpreted as violently as Ezekiel interprets the history of Israel, or does the definitive character of christianity (Heb 1:2) exclude this? What about such reappraisals as the reformation and Vatican II?

4

Judgement
Ez 20:45–24:27; 33:21–22

This section is in some ways an anti-climax. In comparison with the dramatic vision of Ez 8–11, the news of the
fall of Jerusalem is received calmly; the note is one of personal tragedy (24:1–27; 33:21–22). Chapters 20–23 do,
however, bring together several of Ezekiel's main images
of destruction, the sword, fire, blood and sex, as a pre-
lude to the announcement of the disaster which is too
grievous for tears (24:17).

Ez 20:45–21:32. Sword oracles

This section contains a number of separate units put together because of their common image of the sword of
judgement. 20:45–21:7 is an oracle against Israel,
21:8–17 is a sword song, 21:18–27 describes Nebuchadrezzar's final march on Jerusalem and is linked with
a curse on Zedekiah, and 21:28–32 is a sword oracle
against the Ammonites.

20:45–48 is interpreted in 21:1–5, apparently as a
result of mockery, by the prophet's hearers, of his ob-
scurity (20:49). The forest fire, an image of judgement
which occurs in Isaiah and Jeremiah, is interpreted in the
second part in terms of the sword of Yahweh. The relationship between the two parts is close: the green and

dry trees are the righteous and the wicked, the fire will not be quenched just as the sword will not be sheathed, and in both cases destruction sweeps from south to north. Both these images, the forest fires and the sword, occur in other old testament writers, but in Ezekiel they reach a new intensity. As two of the most powerful images for the idea of judgement which dominated Ezekiel, they recur frequently in the oracles of judgement in Ez 1-24. Fire is an obvious image for the fate of a city taken after a siege (cf 16:41), but in Ezekiel it should probably be connected with the role of fire in Israel's worship. An important part of the idea of sacrifice was that the offerings were taken over by God by being destroyed by fire, and sacrificial ritual may be behind the image of the cauldron in 24:1-14. Related to this is the idea of Yahweh himself as a devouring fire (cf 22:17-22), which occurs in Ezekiel's vision of Yahweh in chapter 1. It is also relevant that the temple vision in Ez 8-11 originally seems to have ended with the destruction of Jerusalem by the fire of Yahweh. The vine of Judah in chapter 15 has also been destroyed by fire, and the same fate is attributed to the Davidic dynasty in 19:14.

The sword too is part of the conventional Near Eastern picture of a warrior god which Isaiah draws on when he speaks of Yahweh slaying Leviathan with his sword (Is 27:1). Isaiah also speaks of 'a sword, not of man' (Is 31:8) and Jeremiah treats 'the sword of Yahweh' as a familiar idea (Jer 12:12). In Ezekiel the avenging sword appears frequently in judgement oracles (cf esp Ez 5-6), often in language very similar to that of the holiness code in Leviticus (Lev 26:25, 33, 37). This may imply a formal liturgical use for the image, but as with the fire Ezekiel takes the idea further, notably here in 21:8-17. The rhythm and the way in which the description of the sword is almost lovingly drawn out suggest a ritual of some sort, a sword dance or a curse (a parallel has been suggested in the ritual with arrows in which Elisha is involved in 2 Kg 13:15–19). Ezekiel's use of this material here shows not only the depth of his acquaintance with the traditions and culture of his and other peoples but also a keen sensitivity to the effect of such images.

The sighs of 21:6–7 could be part of the sword ritual, which involves wailing and clapping (21:12), but it is more probably an expression of Ezekiel's own feelings, like 20:49. Ezekiel's message dominated his life; his visions left him overwhelmed (3:15) and his own words horrified him (9:8; 11:13).

The power of Ezekiel's imagination is illustrated again here by the vivid sketch of Nebuchadrezzar, which describes the usual methods of divination. This also seems to be a record of a symbolic action by Ezekiel, like his drawing of Jerusalem on a brick in 4:1; here he draws Nebuchadrezzar's route. The Babylonians had to choose which of their rebellious vassals in Palestine to deal with first. The people of Judah may feel they can mock at these pagan rituals, but Ezekiel replies reminding them of their guilt; as at 17:16–20 he regards Nebuchadrezzar as Yahweh's agent of justice. He insists that this is the final punishment, and Zedekiah, who rebelled and so broke faith with Babylon and with Yahweh (cf 17:19) is singled out for punishment as the representative of his people, 'prince of Israel'. Ammon is the target of the last condemnation as a traditional rival Palestinian state to Judah, which tried to take advantage of Judah's reverses (cf Ez 25:1–7; 2 Kg 24:2).

Ez 22:1–31. Judgement on the bloody city

Judah's guilt has brought judgement near (22:4). 'Bloody city' is the phrase with which Nahum began his

denunciation of Nineveh (Nah 3:1), and Ezekiel uses
it to cover both social and ritual offences. In this chapter
Ezekiel concentrates more than usually on injustices (the
main other place is chapter 11), although his overall view
seems to be one of religious purity and impurity; this
comes out in terms like 'abominable deeds', 'filthiness'
and 'profaned' (22:2, 15, 16). The list of offences parallels that in the legal code of Lev 18–19, and lacks the
vividness and particularity of Jer 23:13–19. It looks rather
as if social injustice for Ezekiel is reduced to one element
in Israel's fitness to stand in the presence of Yahweh's
holiness, and this feeling is confirmed by the simile of the
melting pot in 22:17–22. The main point of this passage
is destruction: the impurities of the nation are collected
into Jerusalem to be destroyed. There is no expectation
of refining anything out of the ore, the usual point of this
image; the whole process is in vain, as in Jer 6:27–30.

22:23–31 is a separate unit, which takes the injustices
of the people class by class.

Ez 23:1–49. Oholah and Oholibah

This is the third large-scale attempt in Ezekiel to reinterpret the history of Israel and find a reason for the
events of 593 and 586, and once more Ezekiel uses sexual
imagery common in the prophetic tradition but makes it
cruder and more obscene. The period is that of the
monarchy. The kingdoms of Israel and Judah are symbolised by their capitals, Samaria and Jerusalem, and
have names which are probably meant to be significant.
Oholah probably means 'her own tent' and *Oholibah* 'my
tent in her', referring to Judah's possession of the legitimate sanctuary. This is in accord with the importance
Ezekiel assigns to the Jerusalem temple, but is not the

basis for any superiority on Judah's part; if anything, it makes her actions worse (cf 23:11). Ezekiel's description of the two kingdoms as sisters probably reflects his belief in the ultimate restoration of the whole people of Israel (cf 37:15ff).

As in chapter 16, Ezekiel uses marriage as a symbol for Israel's relationship with Yahweh, but the picture here allows no room for a mention of Yahweh's love or an early honeymoon period (cf 16:1–14). Instead, the two sisters are unchaste from the start, even before marriage; as in 20:7–8, Egypt is represented as the scene of their defilement (23:3, 8, 19). Adultery here refers primarily to political alliances as a falling away from loyalty to Yahweh and only secondarily to the acceptance of foreign gods which went with alliances; this is the reverse of the emphasis in chapter 16.

Ezekiel's main interest is in Judah, and the punishment of Israel's adultery with Assyria is quickly described. The imagery is very skilfully used. In 23:12 Judah is running after uniforms, but the situation becomes even worse, and she is aroused by pictures of the Babylonians and writes to them (23:14–16). We can laugh here, but the description goes beyond that and the crude details of 23:17 and 23:20 make disgust the only possible reaction. The reference here is to Judah's hopes of Babylon as a deliverer from the power of the Assyrians; it was Josiah's attempt to prevent the Egyptians helping Assyria against Babylon which led to his death. Looking back, Ezekiel sees even Josiah's politics as unfaithfulness to Yahweh, a judgement further justified, of course by their failure. Josiah's policies were all the worse for using the sanction of religion, and Yahweh's disgust in 23:18 may be Ezekiel's judgement on the Deuteronomic reform. Later attempts by Jehoiakim and Zedekiah to throw off the

Babylonians with the help of the Egyptians appear, after this, as total madness or wickedness, and this anger at Judah's contemporary Egyptian policy may be the reason for Ezekiel's severe account of the first exile in Egypt (cf 20:7–8). For him Egypt stands both at the beginning and the end of the covenant relationship with Yahweh as the permanent alternative to being his chosen people, and in 586 Egypt seemed to have prevailed.

23:22ff describe judgement on Judah. The attractive soldiers now show their real purpose as dashing uniforms are replaced by battledress and flirtation gives way to the usual atrocities inflicted on a rebellious vassal(23:24–25). And yet all this, Ezekiel insists, is the judgement of Yahweh. The agents of the judgement are the Babylonians (23:23), but at the very end of the oracle (23:27) Ezekiel returns to the 'harlotry brought from the land of Egypt', another indication of the role Egypt occupies in his typology of the covenant.

Following the main oracle are two further passages, one describing Judah's fate in the conventional image of a cup of sorrow (23:32–34) and an expansion of the original allegory to make a different point (23:36–49). This expansion is similar to the one which follows the main oracle in chapter 16, and shows the techniques of later editors.

Ez 24:1–27; 33:21–22. The fall of Jerusalem

This is the culmination of all Ezekiel's oracles against Jerusalem and to mark the importance of the events the date is given and emphasised. It is the same as in 2 Kg 25:1, January 588. Whether Ezekiel got the date right in his original oracle we have no means of knowing, since pious disciples were quite capable of altering it if

it were wrong. It is quite possible that the original oracle
was undated, and the date added by later editors from
the text of 2 Kings. In any case it is not important.

Ezekiel gives his interpretation of the events in the
oracle about the cauldron. He sees Yahweh's anger with
his people concentrated into the siege of Jerusalem, as in
the image of the melting pot in 22:17–22. 24:12–13
could indeed be a commentary on both passages. The
pieces of meat described are also the parts of sacrifices
reserved for the priests (cf Lev 7:31–6), and it is possible
that that association is relevant. The idea of spilt blood
calling for vengeance is common in the ancient world; an
old testament example is the blood of Abel (Gen 4:10).

24:15ff may not refer to the same times as the pre-
ceding section, and we can say little for certain about the
relation of the death of Ezekiel's wife to the fall of Jerusalem. Her death was sudden (24:16), and through his
grief Ezekiel found the words to describe the comparable
national loss; the words applied to Jerusalem in 24:21
are indicative of the place it occupied in the feelings of
faithful Jews. The significance of the absence of mourning
is that the disaster is too great. Whereas mourning rites
were normally regarded as essential both to the dead
person and to the surviving community, here the order of
things has been too badly damaged for any ritual to be
adequate. It is the end of the old religion. In his reaction
to his wife's death Ezekiel is, perhaps more than at any
other moment of his life, 'a sign' to his people (24:24).
Like Hosea's, his deepest personal relationship and his
relation to the community by marriage were taken over
by his call to be a prophet: 'Behold, I and the children
whom the Lord has given me are signs and portents in
Israel' (Is. 8:18). This model of complete dedication to
God continued to influence groups in the later history of

judaism, and must have been one of the factors which contributed to Jesus' understanding of himself as the obedient son of the Father.

The text of the book of Ezekiel has been rearranged at this point by the insertion of a collection of oracles against the nations as a block in chapters 25–32. The sequel to 24:25–27 comes in 33:21–22, where the arrival of a messenger is recorded. The date of the messenger's arrival is uncertain. 33:21's 'in the twelfth year of our exile, in the tenth month' seems to place it a year and a half after the date given from the fall of Jerusalem in 2 Kg 25:2, 8, the fifth month of the eleventh year of Zedekiah, which is too long for a normal journey between Palestine and Babylon, and the correct reading may be 'eleventh year' in 33:21, which some manuscripts have. There is a similar uncertainty, for the same reason, among the manuscripts at 26:1 and 32:1. In view of the sudden mention of Ezekiel's 'dumbness' at 24:27 and 33:22, it has been suggested that 3:24ff and 4:4ff may originally have belonged here.

1. Is there a conflict for believers today between the claims of God and those of life in the world? Is the question of clerical celibacy relevant to this?

2. On the basis of the imagery in Ez 16 and 22, would you say that Ezekiel had a healthy attitude to sex?

5

Oracles against the nations
Ez 25:1–32:32

These oracles have been collected here to form a section similar to Is 13–23 and Jer 46–51. A surprising omission is Babylon—until we remember that for Ezekiel Babylon is Yahweh's agent of judgement. The nations denounced here are in fact—with the exception of the Philistines—those Jeremiah records as working for the defeat of Babylon (Jer 27:3; 37:5). Implied in the whole section is the belief in Yahweh as lord of the world.

Ez 25:1–17. Oracles against Israel's neighbours

The nations mentioned in this chapter were neighbours and traditional enemies of Israel in Palestine. Ammon, Moab and Edom were situated east and south of the Jordan and are said to have suffered as a result of the Hebrew occupation of Palestine (cf Jg 10:12ff), and hostility continued into the period of the monarchy. In the reign of Jehoiakim Moab and Ammon appear in the service of Babylon putting down unrest in Judah (2 Kg 24:2) and Jer 48–49 contains oracles foretelling punishment of their satisfaction at Judah's fall. The 'people of the East', to whom Moab and Ammon are to be handed over (25:4, 10), are the nomadic Bedouin tribes who were a perennial threat to settlements east

of the Jordan (cf Jg 6:33). In the oracles against Ammon
and Moab the religious character of their hostility is
emphasised (25:3, 8). Ezekiel sees in their attitudes a de-
nial of God's action in Israel, the 'profanation' of Yahweh
mentioned in 22:16, for which Israel, and not her neighbours, is to blame.

Ez 26:1–21. The overthrow of Tyre

This chapter is the first of three elaborate oracles directed against Tyre. That city owes its prominence in
Ezekiel to its being one of the states to hold out longest
against the Babylonians. In Jer 27:1–11 Tyre is one of
the states at a conference in Jerusalem to discuss revolt
from Babylon with Egyptian support, but its island
position and its wealth put it in a different class from the
little states of Palestine and enabled it to resist Nebuchadrezzar for thirteen years, probably 586–573. It
eventually submitted, but was not plundered or destroyed, and a later passage in Ezekiel (29:17–20) takes
account of the limited fulfilment of the present passage.
Tyre was at this period the leader of the group of
Phoenician city-states on the Mediterranean coast north
of Carmel, and her legendary wealth resulted from her
position as a maritime trading power. She also had interests in the hinterland, however, which brought her
into contact with Palestine. The old testament records
contact between Solomon and Hiram of Tyre (1 Kg 5),
and later in the northern kingdom the wife of Ahab, Jezebel, was the daughter of the Phoenician mainland city of
Sidon; her patronage of Baal worship in Israel is probably
a sign of general Phoenician influence (1 Kg 16:31–32).

This first oracle condemns Tyre's joy at the fall of
Judah (26:4), and the terms in which it is expressed

imply the removal of a rival, and probably refer to
Judah's strategic position on the trade route from Mesopotamia to Egypt and from Arabia to Syria. Tyre's
destruction is compared to an attack by the sea: she who
was mistress of the seas will be destroyed by the sea and
left a bare rock (26:3–6). The name 'Tyre' means 'rock'
and 'in the midst of the sea' seems to have been a conventional description of the city; it occurs in Egyptian
and Assyrian records. 26:7 describes Tyre's downfall as
brought about by Nebuchadrezzar as the agent of
Yahweh. The poem is interrupted by a prose section,
26:7–14, which may be a later addition. The ideas of the
early verses are taken up again in 26:15, with the lament
of the princes of the sea. 26:19ff takes up the idea of
destruction by sea from 26:3 and develops it into a
descent into the world of the dead. In Hebrew and Near
Eastern mythology generally the world of the dead was
regarded as being under the earth, and in this case under
the waters of chaos ('the deep', 'the great waters', 26:19)
which God restrained at the creation (Gen 1:6–9). A
good illustration of the idea is Jonah's prayer from the
belly of the great fish (Jon 2:2ff).

Ez 27:1–36. The shipwreck of Tyre

This chapter is an extended metaphor of Tyre as a merchant ship, 'Tyre who dwells at the entrance to the sea,
merchant of the peoples on many coastlands' (27:3).
The description of the ship (27:3–9) emphasises its con-
struction out of the choicest materials from at home and
overseas, and the skill of the Phoenician workmen and
crew. The poem is then interrupted by a prose catalogue
of the trading relations of Tyre (27:10–25), which goes
from west to east across the Mediterranean (Tarshish

is in Spain or Sardinia; Javan is Ionia, Tubal and Meshech are in Asia Minor) and south to north from Edom to Syria and Arabia. The metaphor of the ship continues in 27:26, and the magnitude of the disaster is emphasised in 27:28; all the lesser trading cities are terrified. If Tyre can disappear, anything can happen.

Ez 28:1–19. The prince of Tyre

This chapter shows us the inside of Tyre's splendour. Ezekiel regards it as going with attitudes beyond what is proper to mere man, and infringing the claims of God. The danger of prosperity was a common idea in the ancient world, but Ezekiel is thinking in particular here of Tyre's opposition to Babylon, which he sees as an attempt to usurp Yahweh's prerogative of directing history.

This chapter is also a valuable source for the mythology of the Near East. The 'Daniel' of 28:3 is not the person after whom the old testament book is named but, as in 14:14, a Phoenician hero known from a poem found at Ugarit. The second part of the chapter, 28:11–19, applies to the prince of Tyre a creation and fall story with many similarities to that in Gen 2. The main difference is the richness of the setting, and the fact that the fall in this passage is associated with trade, but these may of course be adaptations to the situation of Tyre. 28:20ff consists of later additions. The oracle against Sidon was probably added to bring the number of nations denounced to the traditional number of seven.

Ez 29:1–16. Yahweh against Egypt

The denunciation of Egypt is in much stronger terms than that of Tyre. Not only are there four oracles in-

stead of three, but the punishments foretold are more
humiliating and there is nothing comparable to the descriptions of the splendours of Tyre in the earlier poems.
This reflects the fact that Egypt was much more important than Tyre in stimulating opposition to Babylon,
and an Egyptian army in fact made an attempt to re-
lieve Jerusalem in 586. Egyptian support came to nothing, however, repeating the history of the previous
century when Israel, against the advice of Isaiah, relied
on Egypt for defence against Assyria. This is behind the
description of Egypt as 'a staff of reed for the house of
Israel', and there may also be a hint of the idea of Egypt
as Israel's permanent alternative to Yahweh, which appears in Ez 20; cf 'recalling their iniquity' (29:16).

In 29:1–5 Egypt is described as a crocodile. This was a
favourite comparison in Egyptian writing, but it is used
here in a very unflattering way. The beast is uncere-
moniously dragged out of the Nile to die, and is left un-
buried, the final insult and injury. It is curious that
Egypt's punishment in 29:10ff is made parallel to
Israel's, a re-enactment of Israel's classical forty years in
the wilderness (cf Ez 4:6; 20:34–38), followed by restoration. This sort of speculation may have been popular at
this period, since it also occurs in Jer 46:26.

Ez 29:17ff. Nebuchadrezzar's failure at Tyre

This passage is remarkable in that it draws attention to
the very partial fulfilment of the oracle against Tyre in
26:7ff. It is the latest dated passage in the book, being
placed in 571. There is evidence for a Babylonian invasion of Egypt in 568. The most striking thing about the
passage, however, is the way it describes Yahweh treat-
ing Nebuchadrezzar as his servant.

Ez 30:1–19. The day of Yahweh for Egypt

Judgement for Egypt is described in the traditional prophetic image of the day of Yahweh. Nebuchadrezzar is
again the agent of Yahweh (30:10ff), and the extent of
the disaster is indicated by a catalogue of the fates of
Egypt's chief cities.

Ez 30:20–26. Pharaoh's arm broken

This oracle refers to the defeat of the Egyptian attempt
to raise the siege of Jerusalem in 587 or 586. It is dated
April 586, about three months before the fall of Jerusalem.

Ez 31:1–18. Egypt as the world tree

The imagery is similar to that in Ez 17, but here the tree
('cedar' is not certain) is the world tree of Babylonian
mythology, with branches reaching to the sky and roots
going down to the waters of the great deep. The image
is appropriate to Egypt's (real or desired) role as a world
power. Chaos follows its fall (31:10ff), and the deep
mourns when it goes to the under-world (31:15ff).

Ez 32:1–16. The Egyptian dragon slain

World disaster follows the downfall of Egypt again in
this oracle. Here the dragon is the mythical chaos-
monster of immense size; its carcass fills the earth and its
blood drowns the land (32:4–6). The apocalyptic poem
is given a historical interpretation in 32:11–16.

Ez 32:17–32. Egypt's descent to sheol

Appropriately enough, the last word about Egypt describes the descent of Pharaoh to the world of the dead,

the antithesis of earthly life, strength and splendour. Pharaoh is sent to a place of dishonour reserved for the imperialists—a final dig at power politics (32:27–28). Edom and the others (32:29–30) were probably added later; they do not really belong in this company, and would be unlikely to be much comfort to Pharaoh.

1. Can we continue salvation history after Ezekiel? Where do we stop?

2. For both Ezekiel and the new testament God's lordship over the world leaves little place for political action by believers. Do different considerations apply today?

6

Re-creation and resurrection
Ez 33:1–38:23

This section provides conclusive evidence of Ezekiel's creativity as a theologian. Having described a God of terrifying and destructive holiness (Ez 16; 20; 23), he now pre-reveals him as the good shepherd (Ez 34). To convey the radical newness of what Yahweh is doing to Israel, he combines Jeremiah's idea of the new covenant with the emerging concept of Yahweh as creator (Ez 36), and finally breaks through to something totally new in the description of the raising of Israel from the dead (Ez 37).

Ez 33:1–33. Introduction to the oracles of restoration

This chapter is an editorial compilation, placed here as an introduction to the oracles of restoration which form the last part of the book. 33:1–20 is a summary of the prophet's task, very similar to chapter 18. 33:21–22 and 33:23–30 are a clearing of the ground before the oracles of hope. 33:23–30 repeats what Ezekiel has already said about the exiles being the true Israel (cf 11:14ff). 33:30–33 is a depressing summary of the effect of Ezekiel's work. Whether the attitude of the exiles changed after his words had been confirmed by events we do not know.

Ez 34: 1–31. Yahweh the shepherd

The shepherd was a common image for rulers in the ancient East, and Ezekiel's attack on the shepherds who fed themselves at the expense of the sheep is one of his most direct condemnations of social injustice. It is possibly based on Jer 23: 1–6, but Ezekiel draws a much more detailed picture of the close relationship between Yahweh and his people in the new age ('I myself', 34: 11, 15, 20). Various aspects of this passage are taken up again in the new testament: Mt 9:36 (Jesus' compassion), Lk 15:3–7 (God's will to save), Mt 25:31–46 (the sheep and the goats), Jn 10:1–18 (Jesus the good shepherd).

The parable is interpreted in the second part of the chapter as the establishment of a covenant, not only in 34:25 with the reference to the 'covenant of peace' but also in 34:24, where 'I, Yahweh, will be their God' is the covenant formula. The introduction of David as shepherd in 34:23–24 is not a contradiction of the close relationship between Yahweh and the people described earlier, although the adaptation of the original image may be a later expansion. It would be truer to say that just as Ezekiel's vision of the future involves Israel in its land, so it requires Yahweh's earthly representative. 'David' is not to be like the old kings, but 'prince among' the people and in close relationship with Yahweh.

Ez 35: 1–15. Oracle against Edom

The main point of this oracle is to act as a contrast to the following one on the mountains of Israel. Edom's pleasure at the fall of Judah also occupies two-thirds of the book of Obadiah's twenty-one verses.

Ez 36:1–37. The new creation of Israel

Ezekiel's picture of the new Israel includes the land as an essential part, and this explains this oracle of consolation to the mountains, in clear contrast to the earlier condemnation (Ez 6). But this use of traditional images cannot be seen as conventional or literal-minded, for it goes with an insistence that the future glory does not depend on Israel's own greatness but on a creative act by Yahweh totally surpassing his previous acts of deliverance. Three times in eleven verses (36:20–21, 22–23, 32), Ezekiel emphasises that Yahweh acts not for Israel's sake but to vindicate his holiness. Deuteronomy had said something similar (Deut 7:6–8), but the measure of the difference between Ezekiel's idea and that of Deuteronomy is the new act of creation described in 36:26–27. Ezekiel can no longer hope for Israel to find the power within herself to be faithful to Yahweh; its ability to stand before the holy God depends on God's own act. The meaning of this passage is exactly the same as that of Jeremiah's promise of the 'new covenant' (Jer 31:31–34; cf Jer 32:37–41). Ezekiel does not use the word 'covenant' here, but his use of the formula 'you shall be my people, and I will be your God', in 36:28 makes it clear that this is what he means. The further similarities in the promise that Yahweh will 'do good' to them confirms the impression that Ezekiel must have known these passages in Jeremiah (36:11; cf Jer 32:40–41). The newness of this act is emphasised by both. Jeremiah contrasts the new covenant with 'the covenant ... which they broke' (Jer 31:32), and both he and Ezekiel make Israel's future relationship with God dependent on a divine alteration of man's constitution. In Jeremiah Yahweh will 'put my law within them, and . . . write it upon their hearts', 'give them one heart and one way' (Jer 32:39), and Ezekiel associates this act with the revolutionary idea of Yahweh's raising Israel from the dead (Ez 37:1–10).

Ez 37:1–28. The dry bones

It is almost obligatory for a commentator on this passage to say that it does not refer to individual resurrection, but to the creation of Israel as a national entity again, as indeed 37:11 says. And yet this critical truism is only half true, for it destroys the vitality of the passage as an image. The story definitely is about the raising to life of men who have died; not merely dead bodies, stinking like Lazarus (Jn 39:40), but dry bones, 'very dry' (37:2). Unless we give full weight to this, we cannot appreciate the force of the image, and its revolutionary nature—it was too much for Ezekiel at first, as his cautious reply in 37:3 indicates.

The new idea which comes into old testament thought here is that Yahweh's restoration of Israel to fellowship with him is an extension of his power over life and the world as a whole. That is really putting it the wrong way round; it was rather by thinking about Yahweh's actions in bringing a people into being that Israel came to think of him as creator. The most famous example of this process is in second Isaiah (cf Is 43: 45). In Ez 37 the basic idea is the same as that in the Yahwist creation story in Gen 2, and the detailed account emphasises this: the bones come together and then receive the breath of life (cf Gen 2:7), all this, of course, at the word of Yahweh.

The idea of Israel's re-creation should not be regarded as a primitive and inferior approach to the idea of personal resurrection. It is much more than a symbol of Israel's reappearance on the world stage. The remark quoted in 37:11, which may have been the origin of the passage, indicates how much a faithful Jew's personal life was bound up with his belonging to the religious and political unity of the people, and the breakdown of Ezekiel's personality brought about by the destruction of Jerusalem is another sign of this. In a common ancient conception, the individual has a full life only insofar as he is part of the community, part of the social community by belonging to a family and part of the religious community by fulfilling the ritual conditions for membership. By an extension of this idea, he is connected with previous members of the nation in a much closer way than we can imagine; not only with the 'fathers' (37:25) but also with his descendants. 'The whole house of Israel' (37:11) is not just the living exiles of Judah and the vanished survivors of Israel, but a unity connecting them with 'your fathers . . . my servant Jacob, they and their children and their children's children . . . for ever' (37:25). Our modern question, 'Individual or nation?' has no application here. This outlook does, of course, depend on there being no idea of personal survival as yet (we have seen the beginnings of it in the distinction between heroes and wicked in *sheol* in Ez 32:22ff), so that this unity of the living with their ancestors and descendants is the only concept of life which transcends one man's lifetime. This approach is perhaps also relevant to the problem of identifying 'my servant David' (37:24). Is he the historical David resurrected, a successor in the Davidic line, or a mysterious figure whose identity is still unknown? The answer is both 'none of these' and 'all of them'.

This idea of the unity of Israel is also the most probable explanation of the restoration of the kingdom of Israel in a united kingdom with Judah. If Yahweh's power over death were to be really unlimited, it would have to include all those to whom the promises were made. Similarly, although Ezekiel attaches great importance to Jerusalem and its sanctuary, his basic model for the people of God is the people of the exodus (cf Ez 20), the united people of the Sinai covenant. For Jeremiah also the new covenant includes both Israel and Judah (Jer 31:31).

Ez 38–39. Gog and Magog

These chapters are almost certainly a development by later authors of various traditions of an attack on Jerusalem such as Jer 1:14ff (cf von Rad, *Old Testament Theology* II, 293–294). These are similarities with the apocalyptic elements of the oracles against the nations in Ez 25–32, but here those elements take over and the clear connection with the events of 586 is lost.

1. Compare Ezekiel's promise of the spirit with what the new testament says. How do they relate?

2. Is the new covenant as described by Jeremiah and Ezekiel an ideal, or has it really happened?

3. Is the difference between the resurrection in Ezekiel and in the new testament that the first is a metaphor and the second a literal statement?

7
The new Jerusalem
Ez 40:1–48:35

Whether these chapters belong to Ezekiel's work is disputed by professional exegetes. The picture of the restoration here is so different from that in Ez 34–37 that some scholars regard this whole section as a later addition; others try to distinguish an original core from later expansions—for one such attempt see Eichrodt's commentary.

The section contains the following material:

40:1–42:20 Vision of the temple with its measurements.
43:1–11 The glory of Yahweh enters the temple.
43:12–46:24 The laws of the sanctuary: duties of priests, levites, prince and people.
47:1–12 The river flowing from the temple.
47:13–48:35 Boundaries and division of the land.

The main aim of these chapters is to present an ideal picture of Jerusalem, the temple and the land of Israel in which Yahweh lives in harmony with his people (cf 43:6–9). The temple has perfect dimensions (cf 41:13–15; 42:15–20) and the tribes each have an equal share in the land, which is limited to the west of the Jordan, the original land of promise. Alongside this are regulations which subordinate the whole life of the city to the service of the sanctuary and make the prince a cultic

official. Two passages in particular stand out as being
connected with the main body of the book, 40:1–4 and
43:1–9, which refer back to the visions in chapters 1 and
8–11, and 47:1–12, which uses ideas of paradise and the
mountain of God, on which Ezekiel has already drawn
(cf 17:22–24; 31:1–9; cf also Gen 2:4–14).

A final decision on whether there is a core of Ezekiel's
work in this section—it is unlikely that he is responsible
for the detailed law of the sanctuary—must depend
largely on one's subjective impression of Ezekiel. If one
is impressed by the connections between Ez 36–37 and
Jeremiah's prophecy of the new covenant, this ideal
sanctuary may seem formal and lifeless by comparison.
On the other hand, in view of the prominence of the
temple in the previous vision in Ez 8–11, and the inclu-
sion of David and the sanctuary in the picture of the future in Ez 37:24–28, it is arguable that some such picture
of the restored temple must have completed Ezekiel's
message. If this is so, however, our interpretation of this
final section must be guided by the theology of Ez 34–37;
we must bear in mind also that 40ff is a vision rather than
a blueprint, and not be led astray by detail into making
connections with the theocracies which have marred the
history of both judaism and christianity.

Ten minor prophets

Hamish Swanston

Introduction

The activity of Israel as a nation among the nations led
to an alteration in the condition of men within the covenant society. The old peasant culture was converted by
the operations of the professional soldiers and merchants
into an urban culture which had little care for those who
could not survive the competition of cleverer types. The
new power and wealth of Israel under the monarchic
rule was attended by new frustration and poverty. Social
injustice became a commonplace in the cries of the prophets against the government.

Of course those in control of public affairs in Jerusalem
knew as well as the prophets to what straits many
Israelites were brought by the royal policies but they
thought the international prestige of the nation and their
own sophisticated comforts rather more important than
the sufferings of the poor, and at once to assuage their
own sense of covenant-violations and to make public
demonstration of their proper care for the things of the
spirit, they arranged for a more lavish celebration of the
temple liturgy.

The prophets, however, though they were always ready
to employ the imagery of the cult, recognised that it was a
further sign of their countrymen's apostate mind to think
that Yahweh could be managed like the godlings wor-

shipped under the greenwood trees. The heaping high of
sacrificial animals was therefore denounced by the prophets in the same breath as the whoring after strange
gods.

The pre-exilic society of Jerusalem, and indeed of the
greater part of the two kingdoms, appeared to those con-
servatives still attempting to live by the old covenant
faith, a society of idolatry and injustice. And though
the royal power was supplanted by the commissioner of a
foreign empire, the exilic and post-exilic sayings of these
prophets suggest that the corruption of Israelite minds
was not greatly lessened by the experience of catastrophe
in 586.

That these writers were themselves able to persevere in
their mission amongst such people suggests that they were
'minor' only in comparison with such splendid men as the
Isaiahs. They performed a major work of social and religious resistance to the unprincipled forces reaching for
power in their society. That this resistance was attended
by final failure does not make the prophets 'minor'. That
those who first spoke these words, and those first disciples who collected their sayings, were quite unable to
turn their fellow Israelites from the way of life which had
provoked their jealous anger for the honour of Yahweh,
does not derogate from the value of the attempts.

Several themes are linked together in these writings,
and an indication of their general coherence may in-
crease their individual comprehensibility:

(a) Yahweh sees Israel to be sinful and, as their rightful
    Lord, brings his anger down on the idolatry and in-
    justice of his community.
(b) The men of Israel were not impressed by the pro-
    phets' talk of judgement because they rested in the

assurance that they were Yahweh's people and whatever might be the case with other nations Yahweh was committed to protecting them. Against this complacent view of history the prophets shouted.

(c) The Israelites were the more ready to think of Yahweh as long-suffering because they had since the age of Solomon enjoyed a humanist culture which persuaded them to be content with a concept of Yahweh as a kindly patron who, from the days when he made kilts for Adam and Eve, had looked after his own.

In their attack on this complacent humanising of Yahweh the prophets took advantage of the new learning in Jerusalem which brought Israel into confrontation with the mythologies of the Canaanite and Mesopotamian storm-gods of destruction. The prophets took over the fierce imagery of this foreign language to present the coming of Yahweh as more terrible than the theophany on Sinai.

(d) Yahweh will come just when he is expected. He will come at the great new year feast of tabernacles. The prophetic irony is to the fore when Israel is warned that the feast of light and of hope for a good harvest and prosperous year will be a feast of darkness, of despair and ruin. Men will have had their day and this will be the day of Yahweh.

(e) The prophets' talk of the day of Yahweh holds together elements deriving from the covenant faith, from the old institution of the holy war, from foreign mythologies, and from their own Jerusalem cult. The day of Yahweh is the already chosen historical moment when the judgement of Yahweh on Israel will be put into execution. The day not only fulfils the past justice of the covenant institution, carries the holy war into Israel's camp, makes sense of the foreign images of destruction and the domestic images of worship, it gives history a meaningful shape and a proper climax as well.

It is with their several interpretations of this meaning in history that any commentary upon these prophets must be concerned.

Book list

Besides the appropriate sections in the *Interpreter's Bible*, the *New Catholic Commentary on Holy Scripture*, and *Peake's Commentary*, there are many interesting things to be discovered from readings of these three widely differing considerations of Israel's prophets:

Bernhard Anderson (ed) *Israel's Prophetic Heritage*.

R. E. Clements *Prophecy and Covenant* (Studies in Biblical Theology, 43).

J. Lindblom, *Prophecy in Ancient Israel*.

And a good book for those who want to see what an imaginative scholar can do with the limited material of a 'minor prophet' would be A. S. Kapelrud's *Joel Studies* (Uppsala, 1948).

1

Joel

Introduction

Joel's name may be 'Elijah' in reverse and mean 'Yahweh is God', but this is not quite provable. All we know of this son of Pethuel is that he saw in a plague of locusts that overran his country an image of the coming disaster, and that he got his fellow Judaeans to fast and pray against imminent judgement.

We do not know when Joel did all this. There is no safe dating of anything by the locust plague, for these were common enough and not usually recorded in the official annals. Nor does the reference (3:2) to the dispersal of the Israelites suggest any dating more precise than a post-exilic year. If a guess at a date for the work's composition is to be made from the reference (3:4–6) to Hebrews being sold by the Philistines to the Greeks of Ionia, then it must be some time in the fourth century, and may be just after 320 when Ptolemy Soter entered Jerusalem (cf Josephus, *Contra Apionem* 1, 209). Certainly the book must have been written long after the final editing of first Isaiah, since the parody of Isaiah 2:4 at Joel 3:10 would be lost to the reader unless the original were well known. It must have been composed, too, just when the apocalyptic hopes of the late post-exilic period were finding expression, for a great deal of the imagery of the book comes from the language of apocalyptic literature. We may conclude simply that Joel is a late work.

The book moves gradually from the original historical occasion of the locust plague, through the liturgical prayers, and the imaginative songs of the great army and the fire in the woods, to the last impressive apocalyptic chant of the upturning of all natural categories on the day of Yahweh.

The various parts of this movement may, of course, have been composed as separate pieces and collected by an editor who placed them in this effective order. They may come from different authors and different towns but the final text has so pleasing a unity of its own that this seems an unnecessary hypothesis. A man may grow in understanding as the significance of events bursts in his mind, and he may find new words for each new appreciation.

A different kind of explanation for the various tones of the constituents of the book is that based upon the supposition that it is the text of a liturgy with set parts for different voices. It does not do to shy away from the suggestion of liturgical origins for scriptural texts, indeed it seems odd that anyone should suppose that a piece of religious writing would survive unless it did relate to the liturgical activity of the community, but it must be admitted that there are not in the particular case of Joel enough liturgical signs and phrases to justify an outright assignment of the whole text, as we now have it, to the temple cult. Some would account for the liturgical elements in the book by entertaining the idea that Joel was written by a temple prophet who had a great number of liturgical notions at the front of his head but who did not intend his work to be put directly to liturgical use. I incline to the view that we have a set of liturgical songs which have been adapted by an editor to the requirements of a literary work meant to be read rather than to be chanted. Certainly the great collection of pieces from 2:19 to the end of the book retains many a tell-tale sign of its origin in the temple ritual.

Jl 1:1–20. The locusts

Jl 1:4. The four names for the locusts may be dialect words from various areas, or designations of different stages of growth.

Jl 1:5. Perhaps the prophet is pointing out here that those who normally do not care much about the country's economic problems, and who simply get on with their morning's drinking, will find that life is intolerable for them as much as for anyone else. Isaiah had seen this disaster coming long ago (Is 7:11). Perhaps Joel is saying, too, that the curse of Moses is come upon the men of Judah, the insect has eaten the vine and they will not drink the wine (cf Deut 28:39).

Jl 1:8. The virgin mourning in sackcloth for her young man is rather like the grieving girl on the marriage bed in 1 Mac 1:26 where a poem of conventional mourning has been inserted. The likeness becomes quite startling when it is noted that the Maccabean girl is mourning because the temple libation cups have been carried off by Antiochus, and the Joel virgin's sackcloth is worn at a time when the libation has ceased to be poured in the temple. It is likely that the stock phrases of post-exilic Israelite lament have been employed by both authors to give weight to their descriptions of the misery of the time.

Jl. 1:13. That the cultic libation had in fact been stopped from a simple lack of wine is just about credible, but if

the priests are to call a solemn assembly of the covenant
folk, and declare a day of public penance, because the
libation has ceased, it is remarkable that there is no
reference to this cultic shortage in the cry of the priests
which follows.

(*a*) *The first cry* (Jl 1:15–18). The general tone of the cry
to be raised to Yahweh is that commonly employed by
the Israelites on days of penance. The first half of 1:15,
for instance, is to be paralleled with Ez 30:2–3, and the
second half with Is 13:6.

The day of Yahweh is in many prophetic contexts
coincident with the day of Judah's triumph over the gentile nations, but here, as in Amos 5:18, it is a day on
which Judah is herself to be judged. The pun on 'destruction' and 'Shaddai', the old name for Yahweh, is a peculiarly literary flick at such a solemn moment.

Jl 1:18. The cattle of Judah share their owners' moods
just as the cattle of Nineveh joined in the penitential
humiliations enjoined by the king when he heard Jonah's
prophecy of doom. Here, of course, the cattle share not
because of the kind of cultic universality at work in the
Nineveh situation, but because the locusts have eaten
their pasture as well as the drunkards' grapes.

(*b*) *The second cry* (Jl 1:19). The pronoun is singular in
this cry and both the grammatical structure and the subject matter of these verses suggest that they belong to a
different situation. They are concerned not with the
locust but with the equally devastating drought. Perhaps
this cry has been attached to the locust prayer because of
the fire image used in Jl 2:3.

When Moses first met Yahweh it was in the sign of the
burning bush which flamed and was not consumed.

There is a reversal in the situation described by Joel, for the people are to cry for Yahweh to come to a land in which the flames have burnt up every bush.

Jl 2:1–11. The day of Yahweh

Yahweh comes from his holy mountain. For men of the Near East mountains are obvious reachers from earth to sky and so are the ways which the gods take to come down to men; in the epic of Gilgamesh the gods live on the Mount of Cedars, in later Babylonian mythology the gods go in procession on New Year's day to their mountains to decide the course of the year's events, and in the Canaanite stories while lesser gods frolic on the high places Baal has his throne on the peaks of Saphon (cf Is 14:13–15). And where there was no mountain for the gods the men of Mesopotamia erected artificial mountains, those towering ziggurats down which the gods might come to visit earth. The story of Babel is concerned with such a ziggurat and the proud attempt of men to climb up to the kingdom of heaven. As at Sinai so everywhere else it was dangerous to go up to the god unless he called a man. The king of Tyre in Ezekiel's fall story (Ez 28) was rash enough to take his place on the holy mountain of God as if it were his right. He got sent down.

The mountain image of the heavenly kingdom was evidently taken over by the Yahwists, and there is an obvious historicisation of this process in the story of the struggle between Baal-Melkart and Yahweh in the Elijah narrative, where the two gods fight for possession of the mountain top (1 Kg 18:20–48).

The mountains of Lebanon where Hittite gods lived are taken over by Yahweh in Ps 29, and Saphon and Hermon (where, according to the Book of Enoch, the wicked angels came down to have intercourse with the daughters of men) are occupied in Ps 89. There were two mountains especially sacred to a Yahwist: Sinai and Zion, and it is this latter, smaller, hill that is taken by Joel to be the place for the manifestation of Yahweh on his day.

This is the mountain that both Isaiah (2:2–3) and Micah (4:1–2) prophesy will be raised on the day to a greater height than any other and will dominate the world.

Jl 2:2. The day will be one of darkness. The darkness will be somehow like a dawn across the mountains and a horror worse than any before or later will come upon men. Everything, that is, will be turned upside down and inside out. The dawn will be dark. Eden will be a desert. The countryside will be devastated and the towns laid flat; as the earth quakes, the sun and moon go out like snuffed candles and the stars cease blinking.

Joel is here writing of the day in just the way it is described at the end of Amos. There Yahweh is 'he who makes the dawn darkness' (4:13), 'darkens the day into night' (5:8), on his day that is 'darkness not light' and 'gloom unrelieved by any ray' (5:18–20). 'On that day', says Amos, 'Yahweh will make the sun set at high noon', and 'darken the earth in a day of light' (8:9).

Obviously both Joel and the author of these passages in Amos have taken an idea from the judgement day of the flood narrative (Gen 6:5–8) when Yahweh is so exasperated by the wickedness of men that he decides to invert his creation and destroy his work so that chaos may come again.

At the new year Yahweh was to come from his mountain to his people, bringing light and life, but on this day he comes bringing darkness and death (cf Am 4:7-9 and 8:11) and instead of celebrating a grand feast the mourning people are forced to put on sackcloth in a hungry land. That grand order of Yahweh celebrated, for example, in the great doxology of Ps 104, where Yahweh assigns tasks to wind and fire and water (Ps 104:4 and 7), gives grass to cattle, wine to men (Ps 104:13-15) and regulates the appearances of sun and moon, bringing about the dawn change from darkness to light (Ps 104:20-22), is now upturned. The psalm seems to have derived much of its imagery from the Egyptian hymn to the Aton sun-disk, and Joel's strange image of the locusts having lion's teeth (1:6), and his reference to the wild beasts coming out to meet Yahweh (1:20) may, like Amos' reference to the lion, the bear and the snake (Am 5:19), have their origin in this Aton hymn which includes the verse:

When thou settest in the western horizon,
The land is in darkness, in the manner of death,

. . . .

Every lion is come forth from his den

Jl 2:12-20. The call to repentance and the reply of Yahweh

Jl 2:12. It is not uncommon for the prophets in the rush of their words to jump from one persona to another. Those who have to maintain their private selves while being both the messengers of Yahweh and the representatives of the praying people, may be allowed some juggling of pronouns, but there may be here a trace of a liturgical recitation of the next sections of the book. Verses 19-20 are spoken by Yahweh in the first person, and so are verses 25-30, while 21-24 and 31-32 employ the third person pronoun for Yahweh. This may be a relic of the antiphonal chanting of these sections in the temple, with perhaps a choir's part at the end.

Yahweh has evidently not given up hopes of making something of his people. The cultic assembly, with the priests at its head, is to come in procession through the courtyard of the temple to the altar of sacrifice.

Jl 2:18. Yahweh now replenishes the corn and oil and wine stocks that the locusts have destroyed, and he promises to keep the unidentified invading army of the north out of the country.

Jl 2:21–29. The song of plenty

All creation has suffered at the hands of the locusts and has been terrified by the threatened upturning of order on the day, so all creation has to be comforted. The song bids the soil and the trees and the cattle to rejoice with men at the coming of the rain.

The reference to the autumn rain strengthens the belief that this section of Joel is connected with the liturgy of the festival of tabernacles in September. And the emphasis on Yahweh's living among his people (2:27) is particularly appropriate to this festival which had something of the character of the new year enthronement ceremonies that neighbouring cultures arranged for their gods.

Amos had spoken of a 'famine of the word of God' (Am 8:11) when the sun went dark on the judgement day of Yahweh. Joel now says (Jl 2:28–29) that the common expectation of the renewal of the charism of prophecy will take place at the feast. The spirit of prophecy will come upon all the children of Israel as a fulfilment of Moses' hope (Num 11:29), and Yahweh will be with the

men as he was when he worked the old exodus miracles
and went with them in pillars of fire and cloud.

Jl 2:30–3:17. The warning song

Jl 2:31. Joel's editor has placed here a fragment that
should keep the men of Jerusalem from supposing that all
is going to be sweetness and light in the future. The
images employed here are those developed hugely by
later apocalyptic writers. These verses may be a prose
refrain given to the choir, for something very like them
was set down at 2:10 and is repeated at 3:15.

Jl 3:2. The nations are to be placed in the dock for their
offences against Yahweh's people. The references to
slave markets (3:3 and 3:6) suggest a date, for this section
at least, in the middle of the fourth century when Jewish
slaves were eagerly snapped up by fashionable Greeks.

Jl 3:9. In the passage 3:1–8 Yahweh is the speaker, and
this is made plain in the last punctuating phrase of
verse 8 with its cultic cry. In the next section the staccato
phrases belong rather to the men (as does the quotation
from Isaiah in its original context). These shouts are
much in the style of Elgar's devils in *Gerontius* and doubtless were as forcefully sung. At verse 13 the cantor singing
the part of Yahweh takes up the text of judgement with a
first person pronoun, and the chorus comes back at
verse 14.

The old warring nations are to be beaten back by the
army of Yahweh, and they are mocked by the satiric
quotation of the well-known verse from Isaiah (Is 2:4,
cf Mic 4:3).

Jl 3:13–14. The day of Yahweh is linked with the harvest
both because of the celebration of the new year feast of

tabernacles, and because it is the time when the locust destruction is being reversed. According to a probable translation, the day is actually termed the 'day of the thresher' (3:14a) and this image provided perhaps the impulse for the cry of John the Baptist concerning the winnowing fan of judgement, and the later parables of Jesus which take the harvest as an image of the final separation of good and bad.

Jl 3:15. In this last section of the judgement song all kinds of phrases are brought back into service. Perhaps Joel's liturgy was framed by notions not unlike those of Wagner, and just as the immolation at the end of *Götterdämmerung* is designed to bring all the images of the cycle to the audience's mind, so these verses are meant to show how the significance of everything Joel has brought before us is summarised at the day: the upturning of creation, the coming of Yahweh from his mountain, the conquest of the foreigner, and the final protection of the people in the holy city of Jerusalem.

Jl 3:18–21. The coming glory

Probably this was originally a separate song but it fits well enough at the end of Joel's account of the coming day and its celebration at the feast of tabernacles.

Springing from the old Jebusite cult of El-'Elyon (see, for example, the reference in Ps 46 to the streams coming from the holy abode of El-'Elyon), the feast of tabernacles was immediately connected with the coming of the autumn rains when 'all the river beds of Judah run with water'. At the temple of Jerusalem there was a wonderful torch-light procession when water was brought in large pitchers from the pool of Siloam and poured out in the temple over the altar of burnt offerings.

The expectation of Joel as well as of Zechariah (Zec 14:7–9) and Ezekiel (Ez 47:1 and 8), was of a spring rising in the temple court on the day, whose waters would flow to give life to any who would worship in Jerusalem. The nationalist character of all this is clear enough in Zechariah (see especially 14:8 where Egypt is threated with a renewal of the old plagues) and in Joel where the suggestion is that the Nile will dry up and the old Edom enemy be destroyed. There is little trace of a universalist hope. Yahweh's day is thought to be coincidental with Jerusalem's day. It will come when the dogs of other nations have had their days.

In John's gospel the image of the spring on the day of Yahweh is taken as a sign of Jesus. He is the fountain of living water (Jn 4:1 and 7:37). Jesus takes to himself the prophets' designation of Jerusalem as the only source of divine life in the world and opens it out into a promise that from him life will flow out for all men.

1. Is it credible to us that the world should end?

2. Do we look for prophets in our own time? Should we expect God to send them to us?

3. Can the country images of harvest be alive for townsmen?

2

Obadiah

This, the shortest book of the old testament, is replete with difficulties for modern scholars. Arguments about author and date, and even whether this small piece was not originally several pieces now sewn together, occupy rather more space in some commentaries than does the discussion of the text and its meaning. Of these matters, highly important though they doubtless are, and one can never be sure when a nicety of scholarship may not free us all from some burden laid on us by unholy custom, I would here wish to say only that (i) it is quite possible that Obadiah the steward of King Ahab (1 Kg 18) is our prophet; (ii) the sections describing Edom's joy at the fall of Jerusalem (Ob 11–14) are not to be dated before 586, and the section concerned with a coming fall of Edom must be dated before the actual collapse of the state at the Arab occupation in the fifth century (cf Mal 1:3, c 460 BC); and (iii) a great many difficulties are settled if we assume that the book is a collection of texts written at quite long intervals, and a great many other difficulties are at once introduced to the discussion if we do make such an assumption.

If a reader is impressed mainly by the references in the book to Edom as a hostile nation, then he will have a clear indication of a date for the writing in the eighth century when Edom was at war with King Joram of Judah and allied to the Philistine and Arabian invaders (cf 2 Chron 21:8ff). Amos recalled these events (Am 1:11), and Joel's reference to the Tyrian deportations belongs to the same period so that this chronology would accord with the traditional placing of Obadiah in the scriptural canon.

If the reader is convinced that the fall of Jerusalem is at the heart of the book and Edom is hated for its unfeeling behaviour at that time, then the writing of the book is most easily placed during the exile, and corroborative evidence may be adduced for this supposition from Lam 4:21f and Ez 35. The evils coming to Edom will then be identified with the Babylonian raids on Ammon and Moab in the course of the Babylonian march on Egypt.

But if the preoccupation of the writer appears to be with the coming fall of Edom then it may be supposed that the signs of catastrophe were already to be distinguished in events, and a late fifth century date may be entertained.

Of course if the book is made up of little snatches of prophetic utterance then we may date this and that section to the period in which each fits most neatly. Some troubles are disposed of in this way. But then we have to account for the general metrical unity of the writing, and unless we posit a very clever editor indeed, this is somewhat difficult.

Ob 1. The prophet (and his companions, if the plural reading of the Hebrew text is accepted) have heard news from Yahweh; the nations have been talking among themselves, and the prophet now knows that they are planning an attack on Edom.

Here and in the parallel passage, Jer 49:14, verbs of

audition are employed, not those of vision. Perhaps this prophet was more readied in his ears than his eyes for the news from Yahweh. Yahweh adapts himself to the quality of his servants. He subdues himself to what he works in.

But if the message comes from Yahweh why is it that the prophet hears it from the nations? Perhaps something has fallen out of the text after the reference to Yahweh, or perhaps the description of the herald summoning the foreign armies against Edom is an aside before Yahweh's declaration in verse 2.

Ob 2. The parallel with Jer 49:15 is not quite exact but these are evidently versions of the same saying. Whether they both derive from a lost original, or whether one of the extant versions depends from the other, is beyond our ascertaining. It is generally accepted that the Jeremiah passage, 49:9–16, is an editorial addition to the first version of the prophet's sayings. A common source in the general anti-Edomite literature of the Jews is quite likely. Similar war-cries against Edom occur at Is 34:1–17 and 63:1–6, Ez 25:12–14, 35:1–15, Jl 3:19, Am 1:11–12 and Mal 1:2–5. Everyone hated the Edomites, and the various dates assigned to the Obadiah sayings indicate how often the Edomites had given some cause for such hatred.

Ob 3. Probably a happy pun is made here on the name of the capital of Edom. The Edomites lived in rock-hewn cities of which the most important was Has-sela or, as the prophet disparagingly says, they lived in holes in the rock, *sela* being the word for 'rock'. The Greeks kept up the pun in their calling the city Petra. There is a suspicion, therefore, that Jesus' pun at the designation of Peter as the rock may have been both an old joke and none too flattering.

Ob 5. Jer 49:9 seems to preserve a better version of this passage. The sense here must be that while robbers make off with the valuables of a house, and crop-stealers take what interests them, when Yahweh lets the nations loose on Edom nothing will be left in the morning.

Ob 6. Edom's prosperity, like that of Moab, depended on the caravan routes that crossed her territory from the oases of Arabia to Damascus, and happily the route across the north Sinai desert to Gaza and Egypt diverged at Edom too. It was this route that the Edomites denied to the Israelites as they made their way from Egypt to Canaan (Num 20:14–21, Jg 11:17). This was a significant stage in Edomite-Israelite enmity.

The Edomites' riches rendered them a likely prey to all kinds of thieves and their history was a series of efforts to keep the foreigner out. Pillaging was their common fate. David wanted, and took, the copper beds of the Wadi, Arabah (2 Sam 8:14) but the Jerusalem government could never quite control the Edomite territory, the tribesmen regained their independence in the reign of Jehoram (2 Kg 8:20ff), and at last the Edomites stood mocking while Jerusalem was sacked in 586.

Ob 7. Some chaos in the text here half-conceals a story of Edom's unhappy experiences of Arab allies; doubtless those who controlled the southern end of the trade routes were always attempting by treaty or war to gain command of more and more lengths of the route. The history of Edom must have recorded many instances of the tent-banquet and the signing of the covenant being followed almost immediately by some treachery. Such things are not unknown today among merchants and diplomats.

Ob 8. Yahweh speaks as he does in the cult, and the message is the common one of the great men being bamboozled. The sages of Egypt (Is 19:11-15) and the Jerusalem temple (Jer 8:8), have been confused and made foolish by Yahweh before, and Jeremiah echoes Obadiah's mockery of the baffled Edomite intelligence (Jer 49:7ff). The Edomites seem not to have been much interested in cultic matters, they sat thinking in their tents and rock-houses and, in just the way that Solomon's quick saws, homely cunning and commercial flair gained him a reputation for wisdom, so the squatting Edomites became famous as the wise men of the east. The first of Job's friends, Eliphaz of Teman, was an Edomite, and he certainly spoke a plain wisdom of experience (Job 4:1ff); and in Baruch (3:23) there is a further reference to the practical sense of the merchants of Edom. It is peculiarly nasty therefore to suggest that men renowned for their wisdom should be tricked by their friends.

Ob 10. The prophet never lets go his hold on the story of Jacob and Esau as the source of the present catastrophe for Edom. The name of Jacob carries with it the favour of Yahweh and the promise of final success.

In verses 8-15 the whole imaginative range is widened as the prophet moves out from the brawls of the southern Arabian tribes and comes to realise the grander effects of the coming of Yahweh at his day. The Edomite incident now takes its place in the great upsurge of history as the Lord comes to wind up all things in his terrible anger against the enemies of Jerusalem, There is a literary balance between the old time when Edom had its day and could laugh at Jerusalem's misery, and the new time when Edom will wake to the day of Yahweh. The historical foundation for this literary balance is the past antic of Edom when the Babylonians sacked Jerusalem. The tribesmen seem to have taken over the frontier-territories from a weakened Judah and to have crept further and further into the kingdom, occupying Israelite territory when the Israelites could do nothing to resist them, so busy were they with the Babylonians.

Ob 16. The coming day of Yahweh will bring down judgements on all the nations, not on Edom alone. They will have to drink the cup of disaster (cf Is 51:7 and Jer 25:15), that cup which will so stupefy the nations that they will not be able to stand up to oppose the army of Yahweh.

Ob 19–21. This quite separate piece of prose is a herald's proclamation of the coming time when the territories of Israel and Judah are united again and their army has conquered all the surrounding territories. The exiles will return and occupy Edom to the south, Philistia to the west, Samaria to the north, and the transjordanian Gilead to the east. This final message of peace balances nicely the battle call of the herald to the nations with which the book begins.

1. Do the pentecostal churches express an element of the true faith lacking in the more established communions?

2. Is the prophets' talk of Hebrew nationalism and its triumph translatable for our concerns?

3

Jonah

A pleasant tale, this, which improves as it delights the mind. The reader is taken on a happy adventure in the streets of the great city and on the deck of a small cargo-boat; he meets a monstrous fish and a magic gourd, and all the while he can identify a little with the timid, querulous and bombastic hero.

The author may not have been the first to tell tales of sea-monsters, but like the tellers of Perseus' rescue of Andromeda, or of the furies of the great fish-god Dagon, he knew enough of story-making to keep the interest of the hearer to the end. It is a well-told story.

Evidently Jesus liked the story. Perhaps he had been told about Jonah and the monster as a bed-time treat, but when he told those who stood round him to go home and read it again he meant them to look carefully at the way in which the old author was large-minded enough to find a place for the enemy gentiles of the great world in the new kingdom of Yahweh (cf Mt 12:39ff and 16:4, and Lk 11:29ff).

Nahum fixed Nineveh in the Jewish mind as a particularly wicked place, and there had been plenty of time since the fall of that city in 612 for all kinds of unhistorical stories of depravity to have become fastened upon the poor old Assyrian capital. By the time our story was written down, say in the third century, almost anything could be said of that long-ago city and be accepted without much malice as the proper description of the scene.

Against such a dreadful city stands our hero the son of Amittai who, it is said with as straight a face as possible, had adventures of a wonderful kind. That the man who lived at Gath-hepher in the days of Jeroboam II (2 Kg 14:25) would have been surprised to learn of these adventures we cannot doubt. But when the tale is so pleasing who will grudge the teller so small a piece of pious fraud?

Jon 1:1. Prophets are often allowed to express their unwillingness to speak in the name of Yahweh; after all Moses had developed a convenient stammer when told to demand that the pharaoh let the people go, but Jonah is not running away because he cannot do the job, he simply disapproves of the whole business.

Jon 1:3. Tarshish may be Tartessus in Spain, the furthest inhabited land at the other end of the known world from Nineveh.

Jon 1:4. Yahweh's greatness and universal power is shewn by his command over that most unruly and dangerous element, the sea. The gentile sailors evidently come from different towns and each has his own god. None of these can quieten a storm started by Yahweh. Jonah, like Jesus (cf Mt 8:24), but unlike almost every other Jew, is so little alarmed by a storm that he can sleep through the whole tossing night.

Jon 1:9. In answer to the questions of the sailors Jonah declares himself 'a Hebrew'. This term for an Israelite is commonly used by foreigners but by Israelites them-

selves only when they are talking to foreigners. It was the
Egyptian term for the tribes and continued after the
exodus to have unpleasant connections with slavery.
Deut 15:12 and Jer 34:9 both employ the term for those
Israelites who had to sell themselves to stay alive.

Jon 1:14. A happy piece of missionary propaganda is introduced here. The sailors having prayed each to his own
god, come to accept the truth of Yahweh and pray to
Yahweh for release from the guilt of throwing Jonah into
the sea where he will certainly drown, and from the
physical dangers to which the storm still subjects them.
To those brought up in a society with Canaanite memories the whole incident would bring to mind the victory
of the hero-god Marduk over the chaotic force of the
watery goddess Tiamat.

Jon 2:1. Yahweh, having arranged a storm, now ar-
ranges a sea-monster. Everything, even the nasty creature of neighbouring mythology is seen to be within
Yahweh's authority. Yahweh has no need to destroy the
monster of chaos, he can find a nice domestic use for her.

Commentators have had fun looking for a fish, a
whale perhaps or a prehistoric creature, to swallow
Jonah, and some have thought that Jonah was picked up
by a larger ship making its way back to the Levant, but
it is more sensible to work within the conventions of
story-telling. If we can watch without question the
monstrous crow as it blacks out the sky above Tweedle-
dum and Tweedledee we should know where we are with
the monstrous fish.

The neatness of Yahweh leads him to land Jonah not
at Nineveh but simply back where he started.

Jon 2:3. A psalm of praise composed originally by someone who had escaped drowning—like the man who cried

out of the depths, perhaps—and inserted here either by the author of the Jonah tale or his later editor.

Jon 2:7. Like the Mountains of Mourne every height was thought by the Israelite cosmographers to have its feet in the hidden sea beneath us.

Jon 2:9–10. The reference to those who worship idols is, after the action of the gentile sailors, a trifle graceless, but perhaps they are already numbered among those who can worship in the temple and offer sacrifice for their salvation to Yahweh.

Jon 3:1. This time Jonah does as he is told. Nineveh is to be thought of as a huge place. No city so big. The teller would stretch his arms out wide in a hopeless attempt to show how tremendous, how much bigger than Jerusalem, for example, was Nineveh. He is, after all, telling a fishermen's story, and telling it about the city that got away.

For those who don't care for stories the archaeologists have measured the walls of Nineveh and set them down in their reports of the digs as seven and a half miles in length. Perhaps Jonah was tired after all his adventures and took three days to limp through the place.

Jon 3:5. The men of the city believe Jonah—just as he had always feared that they would. They ask Yahweh to pardon their sinfulness. King, people, and, according to Persian customs, cattle, all share in the day of repentance.

And Yahweh relents.

This whole sequence may be an imaginative rendering of the description in Jer 8:7ff of Yahweh's sentencing and then, on its repentance, pardoning, a foreign nation.

Jon 4:1. Jonah is furious. Yahweh, he thinks, may well

be Lord of all the elements, having power over the sea and its monsters, and able to sink a gentile boat, but he should not complement this universal power with a universal love. Love is for the covenant folk only.

The notion of Yahweh's grace being opened out for all nations seems to Jonah, and probably to most of the tale's original hearers, to be an emptying away of his love for Jerusalem. There is only so much love to go round and if the gentiles get some then Israel gets less. He feels rather like those who suppose that episcopal collegiality derogates from papal prerogative. If everybody's somebody then no one's anybody. The teller of the tale, however, has a post-Keynesian view of grace. For him it is apparent that we are not to think of a cake being cut up and there being only so much cake to go round, but of an ever increasing cake of grace.

Jon 4:2. The description of Yahweh is identical with that given at Jl 2:13, and both descriptions evidently derive from the impressive scene in Ex 34 when Yahweh comes down in a cloud to meet Moses on the mountain. The teller is both reminding the people of the making of the peculiar covenant between Yahweh and his people, and bringing this people to realise that Yahweh is greater than the covenant, he is Lord of all.

Jon 4:8. Jonah does not learn this lesson as quickly as the reader. We know by now that Jonah has no right to use for himself the great words of the faithful prophet Elijah (1 Kg 19:4). Elijah knew that he was 'no better than his ancestors' and might as well be among the dead because he had run away from Jezebel, but he was ready enough to obey Yahweh's call and carry out his mission. Jonah is simply sulking because he thinks the gentiles are as good as he is in Yahweh's eyes, and he doesn't want a part in Yahweh's mission.

Yahweh, however, is kindly to all, to the Hebrew prophet and the gentile sailors, to the people of Nineveh, their king and, according to Persian customs, to their cattle.

It is tempting to wonder if the plant above the prophet's head, the worm at its base, and the prophet so out of harmony with Yahweh that his disobedience only leads him to sulkiness, is somehow derived from a fall tradition. The narrative has features in common with the story of the garden of Eden in Genesis, and that of the king on the mountain in Ezekiel. But if it does have origins in such a setting these are now so obscured by the integration of the incident within the form of the present story that they must be admitted to be presently irretrievable.

The final section of Jonah is interesting to the christian as a good example of that teaching method Jesus was to develop so mightily. The sequence of the plant incident is dividable, like Gaul:

  (i)   the action of giving and taking away the shady leaf;
 (ii)   the puzzlement of Jonah which is a demand for an explanation;
(iii) the presentation of the event as significant.

Jonah's plant and his puzzlement become the occasion of a salutary teaching. Jesus' actions often startled his contemporaries and divided them into two groups, those who expostulated at the oddity of the action, and those who took that oddity as an incitement to question him. These learnt the significance of the action and so came to understand the divine salvific will for them. This pattern became the exemplar of christian communication. Like the exodus narrative, which comes into being as a reply to the child's question 'what does all this mean?', the shape of the gospels is determined by the demand for an explanation of a puzzling divine activity and the response to this demand in the primitive christian apologetic.

1. What christian values are preserved by the fundamentalist interpreters of scripture?

2. If we allow Jonah to be a literary invention that reveals the divine do we have to look more carefully at all literary works for the revelation of God to us? Is the novel, the poem or the play often a vehicle of revelation?

Do these questions relate to Jesus being the Word of God?

3. Is the fall story in any of its scriptural versions a meaningful set of images for us? Do books such as Jonah, or Lord of the Flies, *by their use of fall imagery help us to respond to the story?*

4

Micah

The prophet Micah worked during the reigns of Ahaz (733–721) and Hezekiah (720–693), but he does not seem to have been much interested in the political events of the great states. He is a countryman come to town and concerned only with the decadent quality of life in Jerusalem. He denounced both the social oppression of the poor and the outward shows of a merely rubricional religion, as being quite contrary to the ethical demands of the covenant community. And he reminded the men of Jerusalem of the holiness of Yahweh that could not be inactive in the face of such provoking wickedness. The temple itself would, like the heretical shrines of Samaria, be destroyed by Yahweh if there were no effective reform movement in the city.

To the certain work of the prophet in chapters 1–3, we may possibly add 6:6–7:4, but not the exilic chapters 4 and 5 which look forward to a new time beyond present horrors.

Mic 1:2. The picture of Yahweh setting out from his sacred home in the heavens and coming down to 'the high place' suggests the arrival of a ziggurat sky-god who, when he came to visit his people, landed at the temple on top of the monument and then walked down to the temple at the foot.

Mic 1:5. The denunciation of Samaria seems to have been enlarged to include the men of Jerusalem, perhaps by an editor working after the collapse of the northern kingdom in 721.

The ruin of Samaria is envisaged in just the terms later used by Jesus for the destruction of the temple, not one stone shall be left upon another. And the ruin will come because the northerners have forsaken the orthodox cult and indulged themselves with polluted rites. The Asherah images of the fertility cult are the outward signs of inward corruption; they are the chief signs of a cultic world whose prosperity is based upon the earnings of the temple prostitutes. The shrines of Samaria are said to be kept going by the monies earned by those lascivious priestesses who join themselves to the worshippers at feasts connected with the agricultural cycle.

Mic 1:8. Micah is going to act out the coming desolation. Like Isaiah and Jeremiah he makes himself a visible prophecy. These prophets were not convinced of the total effectiveness of the spoken word. They knew that the visual image communicated more immediately. In contrast to the golden limbs of the voluptuous goddess Micah set his own stringy toes and narrow loins. And his body, like Yorick's skull, warns the people 'Let her paint an inch thick, to this favour she must come'.

Mic 1:10. Micah indulges here in a series of rough puns, like those which seem to have delighted the Elizabethans, in which merely the repetition of a word or its sound in a different context is enough to count as wit. There are examples of this kind of word-play in the references to Gath and "announce', Beth-leaphrah and 'dust', Shaphir and 'horn', Maroth and 'bitterness', Moresheth and 'bride'. But these are not made purely for fun. Micah suggests that only in his own day can men realise the true significance of these city-names. The peoples have reached the turning-point of history when signs and symbols and names are to be opened up to reveal that which had been meant from their beginning.

Mic 1:16. Every custom is now in abeyance. The enactments of the law in Deuteronomy that the earnings of a prostitute are not to be brought to Yahweh's shrine (Deut 23:18) and that faithful Israelites, other than the designated prophets, are not to shave their heads (Deut 14:1) simply codify ancient and accepted social prohibitions. Micah is saying that the Asherah cult has so overthrown the true norms of Israelite life that the old command against hopeless wailing and shaving can no longer hold. The people have come to the end of civilised life.

Mic 2:1. The overthrow of images and the splitting open of names is about to happen because wickedness has had its full run in society. Now the rich men have time for plots and stratagems, and the poor men slide down into greater poverty as they resort to mortgages upon mortgages, their fields, their families, their bodies being made over to the exploiters. These wicked rich men will in turn, by the balancing plot of Yahweh, feel the full horror of the end. In time the Assyrians will make mocking songs of their distress, and at the final resolution of Yahweh's justice the exploiter will have nothing to call his own.

Mic 2:6. In this section the editor has set down a dialogue between the prophet and the protesting profiteers. These men (cf Is 30:10, Am 2:12, 5:10, 7:16) think that Yahweh ought to be content with their calling him 'Lord' in the liturgy. As a merciful divinity he cannot be as hard, they suppose, as Micah suggests.

Micah retorts that those who snatch the coat off the back of a fellow Israelite are not the best interpreters of Yahweh's dealings with his people, and by their farcical attention to soothsayers of wine and roses they show how far they have lost their hold on reality.

Mic 2:12. At this point, in what is probably a post-exilic addition to the text, Yahweh enters the debate and justifies Micah's hopes of a discerning eschatological division between the rogues and that faithful remnant which more than one late prophet encouraged.

Mic 3:1. Back to Micah's attack on the exploiters. This now becomes a political attack on the leaders of the nation who should know the difference between good and evil. This attack on the chief citizens is followed by an arraignment of the deceptive prophets who have spoken only what they knew the wicked wanted to hear and who, if not rewarded, have resorted to cursings. These prophets are like that witch in *Macbeth* who asked the sailor's wife for chestnuts and, being repulsed, set to work on a nasty spell against the master of the *Tiger*.

Micah does not, like some religious men, deny the possibility of these prophets having access to the world of divine will behind our histories; he denounces these seers not as frauds but as self-seeking money-grubbers. Those who want to hob-nob with the great men will come at last to be as outcast as the lepers who have to cover their lips (Lev 13:45) lest their breath infect the villagers. Micah, contrariwise, because he is empowered by the breath of Yahweh is enabled to speak out against the whole nation.

Mic 3:9. The eschatological vision is completed with the images of the city, built by poorly paid and slave labourers, being destroyed, of those who sold justice in the Jerusalem courts being taken into exile, and of the liturgy of lip-service being silenced on the temple hill.

Mic 4:1. After the catastrophe and the cleansing will come the glory of the new Jerusalem. The nations of the world will go up in procession to the temple feasts, acknowledging the might of Jerusalem's divine protector. Mic 4:1–3 is exactly the same as Is 2:2–4. Probably this is a common piece of post-exilic literature often employed by the levitical preachers to conjure up an image of life in a time of kinship, friendship and peace.

Mic 4:9–10. These verses come from a set of sayings at a time of siege, probably the chaotic days of 587 and Zedekiah's helpless government.

Mic 4:11–5:1. A different group of sayings. These deal with an image common since the days of Ezekiel, that of the nations surrounding Jerusalem (cf Ez 39:4ff). Micah thinks of Jerusalem as tossing and goring all her enemies. The bull image is used of the Joseph tribe by Moses in the Deuteronomy blessing (Deut 33:17f), of the nation of Israel in Balaam's blessing (Num 24:8), of the virtuous man in Ps 92:10, and originates in the old Canaanite worship of El, the bull father of Baal. Baal himself takes a bull's shape, presumably, when he mates with the heifer in one Ras Shamra legend. But Jerusalem is not quite this bull of heaven for the pronouns here are feminine. So it is possible that the image here is immediately connected with that horned goddess of procreation and strength on the ivory panel of the royal bed of Ugarit.

Mic 5:2. Such a horned goddess as she suckles her young son might well be the link in the editor's mind with the Bethlehem saying that he puts here which is concerned with the birth of the coming king. The whole cluster of images of remnant, flock, peace, and the horns of power, come together in this child who is set in historical context as the victor over the Assyrians. The meaning of the child is not to be sought in mere imaginative constructions but in his historical action among the nations.

The importance of Bethlehem for Micah is that it was in this town that Yahweh began the whole process of the Davidic monarchy, and by retracing his steps Yahweh is determining that he will start again. For Micah the return to Bethlehem is the final dismissal of Jerusalem and the court. Micah is rejecting the whole business of the Davidic covenant and the promise of an eternal line, and he is doing this while there is still a Davidic inheritor on the throne. Micah did not have to wait for the exile to realise that nothing was going to come of the Davidic dead end.

Mic 5:5. Seven shepherds and eight princes. Probably 'shepherd' is a synonym for 'prince'. The name of the fifteenth dynasty of Egypt, *Hyksos*, was interpreted by the priestly historian Manetho as meaning 'shepherd kings'. *Hyksos* would seem to have meant simply 'alien rulers' but the coming together of shepherd and king in the account of these semitic kings is significant as an indication of the way in which later Israelites might bring together the two functions.

The progress from seven to eight, like that in Am 1 and Prov 30 from three to four seems to be a Hebrew convention for an oncoming number that is ever increasing and defies counting. Like that of Banquo's sons the line of these shepherd kings stretches out to the crack of doom:

> Another yet! A seventh! I'll see no more
> And yet an eighth appears, who bears a glass
> Which shows me many more.

Mic 5:6–8. A small song structured on two symmetrical strophes. It comes from the post-exilic period.

Mic 5:8–14. Another song of uncertain date, making a fierce point against the pillars of Astarte, and the promises of victory and tall, dark handsome strangers, made for those who cross the soothsayer's palm with silver.

Mic 6:1. Lawcourt scenes in which Yahweh and Israel appear in the determination of justice are common in Israel's literature (cf Is 3:13ff, 5:3ff, Jer 25:31, Hos 4:1, 12:2). The mountains are the witnesses, Israel the accused, Yahweh the judge and prosecutor, conducting his case through the prophet. The history of Yahweh's saving acts is rehearsed with all kinds of odd detail: Miriam and Aaron, for example, occur only here in the prophetic literature. The history of Israel's revolt is rehearsed also until the final cultic horror when the people sacrifice children as if Yahweh had been Moloch (6:7). Micah's final description (6:8) of what is demanded of a good Jew has the ring of a children's school imposition to be learnt by heart.

The verdict is of Israel's guilt, and the sentence is the taking away of that peace and wine in the orchard for which Israel had hoped. Those who oppress the poor and, like Ahab, snatch a man's field from him (cf 1 Kg 21), will lose everything they have and those who made a universal prey will find their families turning against them in total treachery (cf Ex 20:12, 21:15, and Deut 21:18ff).

Mic 7:8–10, 7:11–13 and 7:14–20. Three songs are placed here by the editor to give a sense of hope at the end of the book. The post-exilic writers and harmonisers of previous material could not bear to leave their texts with words of condemnation and despair, the country had gone through too much to be told that worse was to come.

The reference in verse 11 to the rebuilding of the walls of Jerusalem dates this song before the commission of Nehemiah. Perhaps these are three exilic songs sung to cheer the captives as they lived through the delay of restoration.

1. Are there equivalents to the old fertility cults in our society? Was the cleric exact who described Jayne Mansfield as 'the goddess of lust'? Was she right to be delighted by the description?

2. Do we have much faith in those who claim to see the future? Should we have more?

3. Is the imagery of the shepherd still vital in our society? Do we care to be termed the sheep or flock of our pastor?

5

Nahum

This group of Hebrew lyrics is concerned with the fall of
Nineveh, the great Assyrian capital, in 612, just fifty years
after the Assyrians had seemed, at their conquest of
Egypt in 664, to be the masters of the world. The prophet smacks his lip at the relish of the tyrant's downfall.
Here is proof if any demand it that Yahweh is not
mocked. The only message Nahum has for Israel is that
the people prepare a celebration in honour of Yahweh's
victory, and it would seem likely that the songs collected
here were originally composed for such a celebration in
the temple of Jerusalem.

The songs of the Nahum group are evidently not
composed for choral recitation or for the alternating
chant of cantor and congregation. They are rather designed to be sung by a priest while the congregation
listens with ever increasing excitement to the story of the
coming catastrophe.

It is just possible that the second song, 1:9–2:2, was
performed by more than one cantor, one introducing the
divine speaker, 'Yahweh says this', and the other reciting
Yahweh's part, rather like a mediaeval chant or Bach
setting of a passion narrative.

The poems were probably composed near the time of
the collapse of Nineveh and though it may seem sophisti-

cated to suggest that the poems were made after the
event so as to make it seem that the prophet had foretold the future, it is more sophisticated still to accept the
songs as expressions of a blood-thirsty wish for the oppressors, a wish that was not so entirely fulfilled as the
songs recommend.

I would think that they were sung on days of inter-
cession when the news reached Jerusalem that the army
of Medes, Babylonians and Scythians was bearing down
on the Assyrian capital.

Nah 1:1–8. The first song

Nah 1:2. The disordered alphabetical song, though not
by Nahum, sets the tone of this furious piece of prophetic
writing:

'Yahweh avenges'.

Retribution will come on all who have defied the power
of Yahweh and taken up arms against the men of Jerusalem.

The work of Nahum, wholly concerned with wars and
political triumphs, comes very close to falling under the
condemnation pronounced by Jeremiah and Micah
against those jingoistic prophets who employed their
divine gifts for merely political ends. The prophet's name
means 'comforter' and this title may have been given
him by those leaders of Jerusalem who found hope of
final prosperity in his denunciations of the enemy.

The song itself is reminiscent of those old Canaanite
celebrations of the coming of the storm-god Baal. Compare, for example, verse 4 and this Ugaritic song of
triumph:

Then soars and swoops the mace in the hand of Baal

Even as an eagle in his fingers
It smites the head of Prince Sea
Between the eyes of River the Ruler;
Sea collapses and falls to the ground,
His strength is impaired
His dexterity fails
Baal drags Sea away and disperses him.

Nah 1:9–2:2. The second song

Nah 1:9. Like Milton's engine Yahweh strikes but once. The enemies are told of the coming vengeance:

(i) Assyria is warned that a man like Sennacherib cannot stand against Yahweh. Judah is told (1:12–13) that release is on the way;
(ii) Assyria is warned that the cult of the Nineveh gods is about to end. Judah is told to prepare for a temple feast.

Nah 1:14. The judgement on the king of Nineveh may have been first composed as text to be written on some figurine model which was then borne away to a rubbish tip, like Gehenna under the temple rock, in a form of imitative magic.

The whole group of poems is designed to convey a curse upon the Ninevites. The descriptions of the future terrors are in some way thought to bring the terrors themselves nearer. They form that kind of spell, or talk of ill-fortune, against which many a modern man reacts by the primitive spell-breaking action of touching wood. Careless talk or malevolent talk costs lives.

That the fall of Nineveh and the triumph of Babylon brought merely a further horror to Jerusalem suggests that the song was composed at the time of the collapse of 612 and certainly before the Babylonians had shown what was to come.

Nah 2:3–13. The third song

Nah 2:3. This would seem to be a song of the temple liturgy sung by the priests as they heard news of the Babylonian advance. It is a powerful piece with a grand command of the languages of military description and religious invective. There is a fine display of exotic terms for siege engines like the mantelet or battering ram, and common cries like the useless 'Stop!'. And there is a nice suggestion of religious exhilaration at the misfortunes of Ishtar who is grabbed from her sanctuary and her votaries left to the pleasure of the foreign soldiery.

Nah 2:12. The nationalist mockery of the Assyrian lions, who appear so commonly on the sculptured monuments of that culture, becomes a poetic statement of some beauty. The image of the lion foraging for his lioness and the cubs is extended with an almost epic vitality of language until it becomes capable of figuring the whole history of the Assyrian empire as it went far out into the Near East for treasures until its own den was at last destroyed by enemies.

Nah 2:13. The Jewish memory is long. This reference to the envoys of Assyria would at once be understood by the hearers in Jerusalem as a reminder of the humiliation of Hezekiah when Sennacherib's envoys stood outside the walls of the city and, refusing to speak in the Aramaic of diplomacy, mocked the poor king in the vernacular all the listening people understood, and proudly told the men of Yahweh that they would soon be eating their own dung.

Nah 3:1-19. The fourth song

A splendid piece of verse, this. Quick rhythms and a rush of descriptive phrases make a lively denunciation of the harlot city.

Nineveh is not, of course, a harlot because she has deserted Yahweh. After all only Israel is the bride of Yahweh. Nor because Nineveh has amassed wealth through wickedness. But because of the huge influence in Ninevite society (as it seemed to Israel, anyway) of the ritual prostitutes and their allurements. The punishment of Nineveh is according to the coarse terms of popular Hebrew justice. The customary treatment of a prostitute is meted out to Nineveh.

Nah 3:8. No-amon, the city of Amon or *the* city, was the centre of Egyptian worship of Amon-Re, and its civic history entertained the curious notion that all other cities were termed 'city' in reverential imitation of *the* city (cf Jer 46:25 and Ez 30:15ff). The priests of Amon-Re located the primeval hill upon which creation took place as the site of their temple and everything in Egypt was, in Theban eyes, centred upon Thebes. It was therefore catastrophic when Thebes, having recovered its status after the unfortunate episode of Akhenaton, fell to the Assyrian king, Ashurbanipal, in 663. The prophet's song suggests that if *the* city could not at last resist an enemy then certainly Nineveh's case is hopeless.

That the Assyrians could not hold Thebes long and that the Egyptians claimed to have defied the Assyrians on their next campaign does not affect the literary force of the singer's image of the downfall of Thebes.

Nah 3:16. The image of the locusts is developed just like that of the lion, 2:12ff, and the creatures make a good figure for the Assyrian quick money-makers and petty

officials who covered the land but who could not offer an
effective opposition to the soldiery of Babylon. The young
locusts eat up everything around them, and then, shed-
ding their wing-sheaths, fly off to other fields with no
thought of the devastation they have worked. The song
must have been composed at the beginning of the Babylonian attack for the Ninevites put up a very spirited
defence.

*1. Do we approve Nahum's involvement with the political
fortunes of his people?*

*2 What images from the secular world of our time would be
useful in the enlivening of our liturgical language?*

3. Is there enough superstition in our lives?

6

Habakkuk

The triumph expected in the Nahum chants was not as great or as long-lasting as the priests hoped. In 609 Josiah was killed and the Egyptians ruled in Judah. In 605 the Egyptians were themselves defeated by Nebuchadrezzar and Palestine came under the Babylonian government.

At this time, say from 609 to 597, Habakkuk worked in Judah. Like Nahum, he seems to have been at ease within the liturgical forms, but unlike Nahum, he was disturbed by history. He questions events, probing the divine actions for some pattern and enquiring for Yahweh's answers to the problems of his day. Perhaps Habakkuk's sayings should be understood as of a kind with those strange intercessions of modern liturgies which seem to be thinking aloud as well as making a prayer, and take the form: 'O Lord who knowest all this . . . hear our voice'. The recitation of what the Lord knows is really intended to get the situation clear in the congregation's mind.

Perhaps Habakkuk was employed by the supervisors of the Jerusalem cult to ask public questions of Yahweh and transmit the divine answers to the worshippers. Certainly the form of question and answer at the beginning of the book suggest some such liturgical setting.

Hab 1:2. The prophet begins with a question. He takes the initiative in a way that earlier prophets would have thought improper. The question is concerned with social evils and the prosperity of the wicked in a world in which Yahweh's will is supposed to be paramount.

It is not clear whether the prophet is complaining about the oppressive Assyrian forces holding down Judah, or about the rapacious members of his own society who are getting rich through crime and buying their acquittal in the courts. Perhaps both are in mind. The proximity of the army may have led many Jews to think it not worth while maintaining the social virtues when all the world will soon be lost in turmoil.

Hab 1:5. The reply of Yahweh suggests that the Chaldeans are being stirred up against the Assyrians in order that the men of Judah may be released from their oppressors. The Chaldeans had only recently defeated the Assyrians and Egyptians at Carchemish in 605. Palestine was about to discover the likeness of its old and its new masters, but for the moment anything seemed better than the Assyrian dominion.

Hab 1:12. Once the Chaldeans had settled their control of the old Babylonian empire they took to making yearly sorties into the Levant just to show the peoples who owned them. Why does Yahweh allow the wicked to gobble up the innocent?

Yahweh cannot plead, as might a seasonal vegetation god, that there are periods of the year when he is powerless. He is 'the Holy One who never dies', so his power is always the same. He surely cannot lack the will to save the good man? The later Jewish scribes thought this whole reference to Yahweh and dying gods quite blasphemous, an idea better not thought, and certainly better not published, so they changed the text to a weak and inapt phrase, 'We shall not die'.

Hab 1:14. There is a confusion of pronouns in the following lines but it is generally clear that Chaldeans are like successful fishermen, dragging out as many fish as they want from the sea and not caring much for the feelings of the fish. The image is maintained to demonstrate the total godlessness of these Chaldeans; their god is their net. There is not a deal of evidence to suggest an actual cultic service of the net among these peoples, though Herodotus (*History*, IV, 62) says that the Scythians of the Chaldean axis worshipped a sword as a sign of their war-prowess.

Hab 2:1. The prophet takes up his place to receive the reply of Yahweh. Perhaps there is an allusion here to some cultic platform upon which the prophet stood when asking guidance in public affairs. The term *mishmereth*, 'watchtower', is used of the priestly station in 2 Chron 7:6, 8:14, 35:2 and in Neh 7:3 and 13:30, and may well be taken as a specially marked place like that reserved for the king beside one of the pillars in the sanctuary (cf 1 Kg 7:15–22 and 2 Kg 11:14). On the other hand Habakkuk may be employing the quite common image of the prophet as on the lookout for Yahweh's will (cf Is 21:6–9; 56:10; Jer 6:17, Ez 3:17 and Mic 7:4).

Hab 2:2. Yahweh's reply to the questionings of 1:12ff is one which hurries the event. His word makes things come quickly. Yahweh's justice seemed to Habakkuk to be impugned by the easy victories of the Chaldeans. If things could go wrong on such a huge scale, the second question arose of how any individual could hope for justice in this world. Ezekiel was quite happy with the way in which the balance is kept between individual responsibility for action and divine providence, but Habakkuk cannot see how Yahweh's justice is at work. The whole matter is obscure for him and he does not bring in Yahweh to voice a solution. He has no revelation in this matter unless it be that perseverance in faith will lead into life (2:4).

Jerome saw the coming fulfilment of Yahweh's plan in the person of Christ and deliberately translated 'vision' not by the feminine *visio* but by *visus*. The author of Hebrews at 10:38, like Paul at Rom 1:15 and Gal 3:11, takes this text to refer more widely to the fulfilment of the divine harmony in the life of every just and faithful man. These authors have made a transference from Habakkuk's notion of loyalty to the covenant way of life to that of loyalty to a person. This transference was assisted by the interpretation of the text among the men of Qumran who expressed loyalty to the covenant by faith in the teacher of righteousness. The Qumran scrolls include a commentary on Hab 1-2 which is useful on occasion in the establishment of the original reading of the text.

Hab 2:5-20. The curses

Textually there is some dispute as to whether it is wealth or wine that is at the root of all evil done in the land. The prophet may be making an economic analysis of the effects of money being gathered into the coffers of the few, or he may be making an image of society being broken up by the drunken rioter in the streets. Exploiter or drunkard the man deserves a curse. He gets five curses. These curses may not have been composed all at one time. The prophet himself or a later editor may have collected them together at the end of the prophet's career.

It has been suggested that there is in these curses something akin to the Egyptian execration texts, written on pieces of pottery which were immediately broken as an indication to the gods of what was to be done to the enemy named on the pot. But Habakkuk's curses are more general. They are directed against groups of Judaeans and are not composed so much to bring divine wrath on the men as to point out that a man's own actions bring Yahweh's judgement down on him.

Hab 2:6. Curse I. Habakkuk directs attention here to the commonly denounced profiteer who lends out money to the poor and then suddenly calls in the debts so that they have to surrender their pledges. The prophet envisages a time when they will rise against the bailiffs and start a new society.

There is some support for an interpretation of this curse being against the Babylonian king Nebuchadrezzar and his harsh exactions from the conquered countries. The king may be, of course, an example to warn Judaean landlords.

Hab 2:9. Curse II. If the first curse was against Nebuchadrezzar then this would seem to be against king Jehoiakim, for it is very like the doom pronounced by Jeremiah against this king and his building schemes (cf Jer 22:13ff), though it would be stretching things a bit to describe Jehoiakim as making an end to many peoples. Perhaps it is better here also to keep to the notion of a general condemnation of those who erect great houses for themselves by exploiting the labour of their fellows as if they were Egyptian slave-masters.

Jesus employed the image of the stone crying out (Lk 19:40), but in so different a context that it would seem a forcing of the text to make, as some commentators do, a connection here.

Hab 2:12. Curse III. The curse here is on those who build a city on blood. This is the accusation brought by Micah against the builders of Zion (Mic 3:10) and there is no need to look about for a particular oppressor. Those under the second curse feel this one also.

Hab 2:15. Curse IV. This is a curse whose language is more rough and lusty than the others and it might be thought proper to assign it to a different author and context had we not Jeremiah's vision of the cup (Jer 25:15ff) to put alongside it. In that vision Jeremiah is told to make Yahweh's enemies drunk to vomiting so that they cannot rise to defend themselves when the divine vengeance comes. Ob 16 has a similar image. It is not therefore unlikely that Habakkuk could say such things in the public liturgy.

The image is one of riotous drinking bouts much in the manner of the primitive country revels of Hardy's folk. It would seem from this passage and the Gen 9:20-25 account of the drunkenness of Noah and what was 'done to him', that such rough games were no more uncommon in Judah than in Wessex. Habakkuk thinks that the shame of the drunkards will be greatest when they are stripped and the Chaldeans are displayed as uncircumcised.

Verse 17 is out of place and should be put after verse 13.

Hab 2:18. Curse V. Verses 18 and 19 should be read in reverse order so that the curse has its shape restored.

This malediction is certainly against idols and their worshippers, but it is debated whether the worshippers be Chaldean or renegade men of Judah. If the other curses are taken as directed against the Chaldeans then this would likely go with them, but it is difficult to appreciate why a Hebrew prophet should spend his energies attacking Chaldean religious activity unless there were at least some Judaeans who thought themselves warranted by the Chaldean victories to honour the gods who made such victories possible (cf Jer 10:2–9, and the mockeries of Is 41:6–7; 44:9–20; 46:6–7).

Hab 3:1–19. The psalm of Habakkuk

After an introductory prayer for Yahweh, present in his holy temple, to make that presence felt, there is set down a brilliantly imaginative account of the coming of Yahweh. The liturgical setting of this song is made plain by the directions included at verse 1 (the tone on which it was to be sung), 3, 9, 13 (the pauses, perhaps while some priestly sign is given of Yahweh's coming; the second would be a fit place for a liturgical procession of Yahweh's chariot in the temple area, and the third might be at a liturgical march) and 19 (the instruments required).

The song may not have been composed by Habakkuk himself, and the title may simply refer to the collection in which it was to be found. A kind of catalogue reference for the priestly archivist's help when the psalm was put down for the next day's services.

The song is an interesting example of the way in which the old Canaanite imagery was translated for the service of Yahweh. Yahweh comes from the northern mountains to the grand noise of thunder and earthquake. Against him the sea has no power; roaring furiously the waters shake their fists as Yahweh strides and tramples through the sea. Yahweh fires his arrows at the enemy and puts the whole crew to flight.

There is evidence here of a delight in the old mythological images of divine battle and a number of recognisable borrowings from the Marduk story of the god's defeat of the watery goddess, Tiamat. Those, however, who are bored by such Levantine myths, may be more interested in the fact that the Greek text of the psalm has at 3:2 a reference to Yahweh coming between two animals, and that this verse, together with Is 1:3, gave rise to the charming story of the ox and the ass at the nativity of our Lord.

1. Do we want a just world if this means that we as well as everyone else would get our deserts?

2. Is it surprising that often enough the text of these prophetic utterances has to be unscrambled and reordered?

3. If we do not care for the informative prayer which tells God and us what we already know, how would we phrase liturgical petitions? Ought we to ask God for particular gifts or ought we to content ourselves with the prayer 'Thy will be done'?

7

Zephaniah

Habakkuk's psalm presents an image of Yahweh as Marduk, or Baal-Hadad, coming as storm-god to destroy the villainies of the world. Zephaniah develops this concept of Yahweh as the battling divinity but emphasises the danger in which Jerusalem stands.

Habakkuk had asked awkward questions about Yahweh's justice and had contented himself perforce with ignorance of the workings of Yahweh's providence in history. Zephaniah lives among men who would say that Yahweh does not care what goes on in the world, and even that he has no power to ensure the triumph of good (1:12).

Zeph 1:2–2:3. The day of Yahweh

Zeph 1:2. A general clearance is threatened. Yahweh will rid the world of fish, birds, beasts and man. He will make a cosmic spring-cleaning. Especially mention is made of the coming doom on Judah and the capital, because Jerusalem has gone over to the manners of foreign cultures. Though Josiah had attempted a thorough reform in 621 evidently a strange amount of rubbish filled the city still. The men were bowing down before the idols of Tyrian Baal, worshipping astral deities of Assyria introduced by the apostate Manasseh (2 Kg 21:3ff), and looking for favours from the Ammonite god Milcom (1 Kg 11:5; 2 Kg 23:13).

There will be a new liturgical celebration at the order of Yahweh. The command for silence at the start of the sacrificial ceremony is given (1:7, cf Hab 2:20 and Zech 2:13) and the announcement made, as it was to the luckless Baal-worshippers gathered by Jehu before they were butchered (2 Kg 10:25). On that day those who make the mistake, again like those killed by Jehu's soldiers, of wearing foreign fashions and thus advertising their devotion to foreign gods, will find themselves unfortunately conspicuous.

Zeph 1:9. On that day those who leap over the step are also to be punished. It is not entirely clear who these light-footed persons are. Perhaps they are like the worshippers of Baal described in the account of Elijah on Mount Carmel, who bent the knee and performed some hopping dance for Baal-Melkart; perhaps there was some superstition reflected in the hop, like the first-footing, or the carrying of the bride over the thresh-hold; or perhaps there were men who took over a farmer's property against his will and skipped the process of law.

Zeph 1:10. That the prophet sees sin everywhere is brought out by this list of sectors of Jerusalem and the cries of the wicked on that day which he hears in imagination. Soon real screams will be heard. Zephaniah has with some relish developed the references in Am 5:18, Is 13:6, and Ez 7:5, to this terrible judgement day, and the imaginative force of his writing makes it improbable that he was thinking of any destruction other than the great eschatological catastrophe.

Zeph 2:4–3:8. The oracles against the nations

1 *Against the men of the West*. Four of the old five towns of the Philistine confederation survived to Zephaniah's time and to these he promises ruin. The Cherethites were Cretans and the ancestors of the Philistines who came on raids from their Aegean camps (cf 1 Sam 30:14).

The reference to a restoration of the humble remnant of the men of Judah is a post-exilic addition and should be ignored.

2 *Against the men of the East*. Moab and Ammon were always bickering with Judah in small border wars, and doubtless told nasty enough tales of the men of Jerusalem to warrant the bawdy libel of Gen 19:30ff to which Zephaniah now none-too-obviously refers.

3 *Against the men of the South*. This fragment is addressed not only to the Ethiopians themselves but also to the Egyptians who were ruled from 712 to 663 by the Ethiopian xxv dynasty. Probably this oracle is connected with the great defeat of Egyptian forces at Carchemish in 605.

4 *Against the men of the North*. The oracle against the Assyrians seems (cf 2:15) to have been composed, or at least edited, after the collapse of the nation in 612. Though it may look from the map as if the Assyrians were an eastern enemy, the invading armies from Nineveh always came down from the north into Palestine on their raiding campaigns. The animals named are all wild creatures whose presence suggests that the site of the city has reverted permanently to primitive wilderness.

5 *Against Jerusalem*. After the compass points of the world have been cursed, Zephaniah penetrates to the centre of his society. Following the example of other

Hebrew prophets, he lists those various elements in power in Jerusalem who are responsible for the coming disaster. The princes are roaring lions and the judges wolves, the town is already that wilderness that Nineveh will become. Zephaniah is simply making plain by such imagery the reality within Jerusalem's appearances. Punishment must come. But it is a cleansing, redemptive, atoning punishment, for it leads into the promise of the good life of men before Yahweh.

Zeph 3:9–20. The promise

Like Isaiah in the temple when he receives his vocation, the whole nation is to be given clean lips so that everyone may proclaim the good news of Yahweh, and call out his name in the cult, and lead the peoples of the world to a share in the universal praise of Yahweh.

Zeph 3:12. Zephaniah must, I think, be allowed the credit of understanding as early as anyone in Israel's history that the coming golden age will be for any and all who will serve Yahweh.

Zeph 3:14. The servants of Yahweh will sing a song of his triumph and their happiness at the festival. The editors thought it proper that even the prophet of doom should have his work completed by a popular song of rejoicing.

1. What do we think happens 'after' the day of Yahweh's judgement?

2. Is any punishment redemptive? Do we punish others for the reasons we suppose God punishes men?

8
Haggai

Haggai is the first of the post-exilic prophets and this at least makes it possible to read his work as a working unity. There is no need here to worry about whether threats of calamity and promises of redemption have been added by a later editor, for editor and author will be working with the same concepts and the one will not distort too much the intention of the other, however he may upset the literary patterns of the writing.

Haggai writes after the edict of Cyrus in 538 had allowed the restoration of the Jerusalem community, and after the establishment of old king Jehoiachim's grandson, Zerubbabel, as Persian commissioner for Jerusalem in 520, or thereabouts. The appointment of this young man and the upheaving of the world during the revolts at the accession of Darius I in 522, encouraged Haggai to speak out for the rebuilding of the temple in preparation for a new day. By 515 the building work was completed. Haggai must have been mighty pleased with the effect of his preachings.

If we may suppose the introduction to each prophecy to be historically accurate, and not simply the work of some editor tidying up the text, then we may say that the prophecies were all delivered between August and December 520, but there is no certainty about when they were written down or how much editorial work has been done on them.

Like Zephaniah, Haggai is concerned with the day of Yahweh. But his concept of this day is quite different from that of Zephaniah, for he links the coming of the new thing with the restoration of the full Jerusalem liturgy. The older prophet had been concerned with social justice as a sign of the people's willingness to serve Yahweh, but now they were all so much concerned with material prosperity that it was more appropriate, Haggai thought, to ask them to sacrifice money for the rebuilding of the temple as a sign of their service to Yahweh.

To those who said that the economic recovery of Judah was so uncertain that it was not yet time for such a great building scheme, Haggai replied that since material prosperity is in the hand of Yahweh they would have a more secure economic position if they paid some attention to his interests. Out of the very materialism of the day Haggai plucked a persuasive for the people to join Yahweh. Haggai made of his own time an era of the promise as much as if it had been the holiest years of the world.

That Haggai did not think that the mere putting of one stone upon another would bring in the golden world can be seen in his acknowledgement (2:3) that the new temple did not look much. Out of such smallness Yahweh would work a big thing, a transformation of the world, the temple would be the point of growth for the kingdom.

If the kingdom is to be universal then surely all men may contribute to the building and take part in its cult. Certainly the economic argument must favour spreading the cost among the foreign soldiers on the street corners and the Samaritans in the fields. Haggai would have none of this. Only those who forsook all other gods and followed Yahweh alone could have a share in the covenant cult. He was however ready enough for the time when the nations would give up their idols and serve Yahweh. The struggle was for a pure service from Jew and gentile, and might well be a tremendous struggle, but the certain end was a universal peace centred on the presence of Yahweh in the Jerusalem temple.

Hag 1:1. Perhaps Haggai came back with Zerubbabel from Babylon, and together they planned to goad Joshua into action, or perhaps Haggai and Joshua waited for Zerubbabel's arrival to make a new start in their efforts to have the temple rebuilt.

Hag 1:6. *The first message.* Haggai says simply that those who argue that economic matters must come first have not much evidence to support their case. For all their care of the economy things seem to be in a great muddle. He suggests that if the liturgy is renewed for all the people then they will have a greater sense of community and will work together in the fields. There may be a reference here to economic inflation; there is certainly an early reference to coinage as the common change between citizens.

Hag 1:8. That the men have only to fetch wood suggests that the stone frame of the building was rebuildable from the masonry lying on the site. It may be that the structure needed only a roof to be usable.

Hag 1:12. The people are here referred to as 'the remnant'. The use of this term here may mean that Haggai's original appeal to the whole nation has been edited so that it now reads as a reference in line with the late orthodox view expressed in Ezra-Nehemiah, that only those who endured exile may build the temple.

Hag 1:13. *The second message.* The rallying cry of the old liturgy 'I am with you' may be used here to encourage the people in the building of the temple.

Hag 2:2. *The third message.* The solemnity of the message is brought out by the formal announcement of the recipients, the governor, the priest and the holy remnant.

Hag 2:3. There is a rhetorical element in Haggai's question about the memories his people have of the first temple. Few of them could have any clear recollection of a time before the exile, seventy years before. But I suppose that tales of the grandeur of the past were common enough.

It is clear that the great cries 'Yahweh speaks' and 'I am with you', and the mythological description of Yahweh's shaking of the skies and sea come from a cultic context. Perhaps the messages are preserved by the priest Joshua.

Hag 2:7. *The fourth message.* There is some confusion of the text but it would appear that there is a separate little oracle here. The image has changed to one of precious metals and there is a disturbing equation of Yahweh's glory with the metal glory.

Hag 2:9. *The fifth message.* Yahweh now says that the new glory is connected with the gift of peace.

Hag 2:10. *The sixth message.* The ecclesiastical interests of the editor are discernible from the introduction. The conversation of the prophet with Yahweh is concerned with a question of cultic purity. Haggai goes to the priest and asks his question. The conversation that follows has gone through several stages of editorial working:

(i) Originally Haggai made a point like that of the first message: if the people neglected the cult the resulting disease of life would affect their whole society.

(ii) The text was adapted to the situation after the rebuilding of the temple. It now makes plain that simply offering the cultic sacrifices will not make the people Yahweh's friends. Their hands and hearts must be clean.

(iii) In the later conditions of Ezra and Nehemia the oracle was adapted to apply to those descendants of foreign marriages who wished to have a part in the temple liturgy. The returned exiles wanted total control of the temple, and they laid down rules of political and ritual purity which prevented the mixed peoples of Samaria who had collaborated with the occupying forces of Assyria from having a share in the government of Jerusalem. Haggai was therefore represented as thrusting out the Samaritans who did not possess the necessary cultic credentials.

Hag 2:15. *A seventh message, or perhaps a loose end of the second message.* Haggai represents Yahweh as announcing a perfect complement of liturgical service and prosperity. Once upon a time the harvests failed and the weather was awful. This was the time when the temple lay derelict. The cultic cry 'Yahweh speaks' was heard. Men rebuilt the temple. Now the barns are filled with grain, and fruit loads the orchard trees.

Verse 17b is slipped in, quite inappropriately, from Am 4:9, because a scribal copyist could not understand

the muddled grammar of the Haggai text. Pay no heed
at all to the declaration that the people still would not
turn to Yahweh. The whole point of this message is that
the present prosperity is the direct result of their having
turned to Yahweh.

Hag 2:20. *The eighth message.* The beginning of this message is couched in highly mythological terms taken from
the Ugarit stories of Baal-Hadad. But these are not the
only resources Haggai has for his presentation of Yahweh.

Hag 2:22. That Yahweh is the Lord of history and not
simply the figure of story and chant is emphasised by the
references to his overthrowing horses and riders, which
reminds his hearers of the exodus song of the Reed Sea
crossing (Ex 15:1), and to the enemies falling on each
others' swords, which reminds them of the panicked
Midianites of the Gideon saga (Jg 7:22), and the
maddened Philistines of Saul's campaign at Michmash
(1 Sam 14:20).

Hag 2:23. As the three cultic cries 'Yahweh Sabaoth
speaks' are heard it is almost as if Haggai were creating
an accession scene for Zerubbabel so that his prophetic
word would bring about the event for which he obviously hoped. Zerubbabel is designated the signet ring
of Yahweh. This was a title denied Coniah, the son of
Jehoiakim by Jeremiah (Jer 22:24). The signet ring of
the king carried his full authority. It was used by his
substitutes to confirm that their actions were the royal
actions. Jezebel, for example, procured official help in
her plot against Naboth by the use of the king's signet
ring (1 Kg 21:8), and Tamar holds Judah to his word
by presenting his ring as a firm pledge of his authority
(Gen 38:18 and 38:25). So Zerubbabel is in this final

message envisaged as carrying with him in the new day the full authority of Yahweh.

It is evident that Haggai expected Zerubbabel to be the prince of the day. He got this wrong of course. Zerubbabel did not become king. He was not the destined anointed one of Yahweh. But Haggai's mistake is the right sort of mistake. He did at least see that any notion of Yahweh's rule has to be capable of actualisation among the men we now know. Yahweh's rule is as much connected with the cabinet ministers and market gardeners of Zerubbabel as with the divine counsellors and fertility goddesses which other prophets thought it proper to introduce in their descriptions of Yahweh's triumph.

1. Do we associate the day of judgement with a liturgy?

2. Are all ills economic ills?

3. What sources of quotation are open to the man who would fire a modern audience with delighted recognition?

9

Zechariah I

Introduction

Linked with Haggai in Ezra (5:1 and 6:14) Zechariah seems to have been a member of a priestly family and to have been much interested in the rebuilding of the temple. But he was no mere cultic official. His visions are of a strange and violent kind.

In the central section of the prophet's work, 1:7–6:15, he is concerned with the place of the returning exiles in the coming kingdom, and he sets forth eight visions and their interpretations. The visions have obviously been put into literary shape by the prophet, and then reorganised by an editor, and this edited work was then lengthened by the addition of the material after chapter 8. The final additions are dealt with in this commentary as part of a complex which includes our book of Malachi and are not part of the present business.

The pattern of each of the eight accounts is thuswise:

(a) 'I saw' or 'he shewed me' some image.
(b) A heavenly being comes to the seer.
(c) A dialogue takes place between the heavenly being and the seer which makes all plain to Zechariah.
(d) An explanation is offered which makes the meaning plain to the hearer or reader.

Zechariah takes it for granted that the proper mode of revelation is the vision to the eye and not the word to the ear. Like Isaiah and the sanctuary angels (Is 6:1ff), Amos and the basket of fruit (Am 8:1f), and Ezekiel and the chariot (Ez 1:4ff) Zechariah sees the truth of Yahweh and wants others to see it. The words certainly have to be used, but the words are quite secondary to the vision that is given by Yahweh.

It is important that the vision be *given*. The sophisticated images of Athena, Herakles or Iolaos made by the great sculptors of Greece for the Delphic sanctuary, precisely because they are made, reveal nothing, but the visions that came to men of the Levant could tell something of the divine because they were a free gift from the gods.

The Egyptians cherished stories of dream-visions of Amon to Amen-hotep II, of the appearance of Amen-em-het I to his son, and of the sphinx god Harmakhis to Thut-mose IV, and delighted in the legend of the possessed princess, and they had a term that could mean according to context 'message of truth', 'dream' or 'vision'. The Assyrians, too, had a proper respect for the vision. Gudea, the great leader of Lagash, spent a great deal of energy elucidating the precise meaning of his vision of Ningirsu, and was rewarded by a second vision of the god. Dumuzi, the shepherd of Erech, was equally careful to get an interpretation of his vision of the galla demons of death. The epic of Gilgamesh, in both the Assyrian and Old Babylonian versions, has a long section devoted to the hero's dream of the wild man Enkidu and the determinative effect it has on his career, and Enkidu himself has a dream of the great gods Anu and Enlil and their decreeing his death, which inexorably follows.

Sometimes a puzzled man might deliberately seek such a revealing dream by going to sleep a night in the sanctuary of his god. Greeks as well as Egyptians and Assyrians did this, and it would seem that Solomon was following just such a procedure when he went to the old Gibeon shrine at the beginning of his reign (1 Kg 3:4f).

Jewish tradition retained several stories of the divine appearing in a dream. Yahweh made Sarah's case clear in a dream to Abimelech of Gerer (Gen 20:3), he revealed the future to Jacob with the ladder dream (Gen 28:10f) and the livestock dream (Gen 31:10f), and he told Aaron that dreams are the usual means he employed to communicate with men (Num 12:6–7). Zechariah's dreams are an important phase in the tradition of dreams and visions which reached a scriptural climax in the apocalyptic visions of the Book of Revelation.

The collection is prefaced by Yahweh's warning that unless men learn now they will suffer the fate of their ancestors and all be lost, and by a record that the people did turn back in repentance when they heard of the visions.

Zech 1:7–17. Vision 1. The horsemen

The horsemen belong to a patrol sent by Yahweh, after the manner of Persian rulers, to discover what is going on in his kingdom. Yahweh will remedy the evils reported to him, so men have no need to put their trust in fragile human policies. The horsemen are simply a useful image of watchfulness and should not be burned with significances read back upon them from Rev 6.

The myrtle was one of the trees used for the erection of the booths at tabernacles (Neh 8:15), and was used as a symbol of Yahweh's restorative power (Is 41:9 and 55:13) so it was a propitious beginning to the vision. It is doubtful whether Zechariah knew that the myrtle was sacred to Venus and a symbol of love, but certain that he had no wish to raise thoughts of that goddess here.

Zech 1:18–21. Vision 11

The bull's horn is a symbol of great power (cf Hannah's prayer, 1 Sam 2:1, and David's song, 2 Sam 22:3), so probably Zechariah is referring to the world powers who at various times have occupied Palestine. In Daniel (8:20) there is a reference to the kings of Media and Persia as 'horns' and Jeremiah (48:25) speaks of the 'horn of Moab'.

Zech 2:1–5. Vision 111

To the account of the man with the measuring line and the prophecy that Jerusalem will be so rich in men and cattle that her walls will be unable to contain them some isolated sayings have been added. The call to Zion to rejoice has a liturgical origin, but of the rest nothing much can be said except that they contain the first scriptural reference to the 'holy land'.

Zech 3:1–10. Vision 1v

This is evidently a different kind of vision from the first three since it is concerned with an historical and not a symbolic personage. Satan, the accuser of Job, stands to prevent Joshua's entry into the city of Yahweh, and this city is both the present and the new Jerusalem. The priest, snatched from disaster, represents the Jewish people, rescued from the exile. Joshua, whose cleansing and dressing in new vestments contrasts with the be-miring of the faithless priests of Mal 1:3, is clothed in the robes of the Jerusalem high priest and the ritual turban or mitre described in the rubrics of Ex 28. The turban was of wound linen and had a gold medallion attached at its front on which was engraved 'Holy to Yahweh'. It is not quite clear how it was so, but this turban and its inscription were thought to load the high priest with personal responsibility for all involuntary ritual imper-fections committed by the congregation and other sanc-tuary persons. The angel's words to Joshua may be an assurance that all the imperfections which thus rested on the high priest have been taken away. The situation is therefore one of redemption and beginning again. The priest is given charge of the temple and promised free access to the heavenly courts. His prayer will always be heard.

The stone with seven eyes is most probably a pectoral, not so elaborate as that described in the Exodus rubrics (Ex 28:15ff) but having the same significance. The tur-ban was a sign of responsibility, the pectoral was a sign of mediation. The priest when he puts it on is to realise that he brings the whole community with him when he walks to meet Yahweh (cf Ex 28:29).

The concluding verses about the Branch may be spo-ken by Yahweh or by the prophet to the assembled priests, and offer simply a conventional promise of the new era.

The scene of the priest subjected to accusation and then presented to the people as their justified leader may have some historical connection with the warring factions among the post-exilic citizens who were forever resorting to accusations of impurity based on a man's having eaten in Babylon or supped with the men of Samaria, but it is not necessary to look for such an historical occasion for this vision. Cultic contexts would account for all the elements of the scene.

In the 125th chapter of the Egyptian *Book of the Dead* there is a ritual in which the dead man coming to judgement recites before the great god Osiris a 'negative confession' of all the wickednesses he has not committed, is then clothed in clean garments and anointed with oil, and finally ushered into the sanctuary as a member of the household of Osiris. This is a scene of some striking likenesses to the Joshua cleansing, but not of such strikingness as the Akkadian myth of Adapa.

The story of Adapa, like that of Gilgamesh, is of man's losing the gift of immortality by a piece of folly. The priest Adapa, whose name has the same root as 'Adam', on a fishing expedition for the god Ea has broken the wing of the south wind, and is summoned before Anu the lord of heaven. Adapa comes to the gate of heaven dressed in mourning rags, and the god hearing his excuse acknowledges Adapa as 'the blameless, the clean of hands, the ointment priest, the observer of rites', and clothes him in the high priest's robe, bidding him go back to the city of Eridu to perform his ritual.

With this Akkadian cultic myth we should hold in mind atonement ritual of the Marduk festival in Babylon when at the new year the king, standing stripped of his sceptre, ring, sword and crown, protested his loyalty to the god. He was hit on the face and lugged by the ears 'till the tears came' in expiation of every sin of the people. He was then declared innocent of all offence against the god and clothed again in his royal robes and promised a prosperous year of stupendous harvests.

The two Mesopotamian rituals are concerned with the justification and enrobing of a man who has been accused of sins, and it is likely that some ceremony of this kind performed in the Jerusalem cult gave an impulse to the imagery of Zechariah's vision. With this vision we ought perhaps to take the ceremonial crowning of Joshua (6:9f).

Zech 4:1–14. Vision v

Joshua is joined here with Zerubbabel as the anointed guardians of Yahweh's order. Though the details of the design of the candelabra are difficult to reconcile with the suggestion that the image is taken from the temple seven-branched candlestick, it seems sensible to link them. There may be some connection with an astrological interpretation of the seven planets as the eyes of the sun-Yahweh in the universe.

The text of the vision is interrupted in order to include some enthusiastic sayings about Zerubbabel. The prophet is anxious that the work of the commissioner and the high priest for the rebuilding of the temple shall receive every encouragement.

With this vision the reader should take the Zerubbabel saying of 6:12–14.

Zech 5:1–4. Vision vi

Compared with the scroll of Ezekiel (Ez 2:9), or any other, this scroll is huge. It has the dimensions of the entrance of Solomon's temple (1 Kg 6:3) and perhaps the prophet had this image in mind after a reading of the law's curses in the temple court at some restoration ceremony.

Zech 5:5–11. Vision VII

The girl in the jar is revealed when the lid is taken off, like some dancer in a Levantine night-club, to be the wicked Babylonian whore.

Zech 6:1–14. Vision VIII

This vision has evident affinities with the first vision, and it is possible that both, like the planet vision of 4:1ff, derive their imagery from an old sun-god cult. Perhaps Jachin and Boaz, the two bronze pillars of Solomon's temple, were cultic representations of the bronze mountains of a divine home, and Zechariah is there thinking of the Jerusalem temple as the home of Yahweh from which messengers will be sent out to the world.

The concept of the divine chariots and their horsemen, best known to us in the story of Phaeton, has all kinds of mythic and cultic ancestry, and appears in Hebrew writings at the ascent of Elijah who, as he climbs the sky in the fiery chariot, is called 'the chariots of Israel and the horsemen thereof' (2 Kg 2:12).

Zech 7:1–8:23. Various isolatable sayings

Zech 7:1ff. Messengers come to the Jerusalem priests asking whether, since the fast was instituted as sign of mourning for the destruction of the temple, it ought to be continued when the temple is rebuilt. The prophet takes advantage of the question to point out that the Israelites do not really care much for Yahweh whatever fasts or feasts they observe, and they had better look at history again to see what happened to those who forsook Yahweh's law.

Zech 8:1ff. However, Yahweh says to those who are really making an effort to serve him that he is coming back to make Jerusalem a greater city than before. The terrible conditions of the exile and the occupation are over and a new thing begins.

Zech 8:19. So the answer to the original question can now be given: the fasts are certainly to be turned into feasts for those who serve Yahweh in their hearts, and Jerusalem will become the glad centre of a universal liturgy. The conventions of post-exilic optimism which led into the wilder hopes of the apocalyptic movement can be read here.

1. Do our dreams influence our actions—other than sending us rushing to an analyst?

2. Does it matter that there are pagan parallels to the ideas presented in these prophets?

3. Now that we have seen men on the moon is it possible to recapture the sensations of those who shaped a worship of the sun and moon and planets?

10

Three oracles: Zechariah II and III and Malachi

Introduction

The two oracles of Zec 9–14 are not by the author of Zec 1–8, nor are they by one other author. 12:1–13:6, for example, is clearly not written by the author of 14. It is best to think of these chapters as representing, together with those now preserved under the Malachi title, a sizeable collection of prophetic sayings whose origin and provenance is not apparent, but which were arranged by some early editor so that he created a neat set of twelve 'minor prophets'.

The two oracles attached to Zechariah are concerned not with the reassurance of those returning from exile but with the horrors that will occur before the final coming of Yahweh.

The third oracle is perhaps more obscure for the modern reader. Of 'Malachi' nothing is known. He has no legend in Jewish folk-lore, and probably his name is not proper but simply the word for a messenger which occurs at 2:7 and 3:1. This oracle is evidently written after the restoration of the temple services, long enough after, indeed, for the priests to be already tired of the ritual burdens. Since the priestly code of Ezra is not referred to as a rule for the temple officials, it must have been written before Ezra's work and, since foreign marriages are going on without let, the book must have been composed before Nehemiah's reforms were operating. So the date of composition must be quite a long time after 515 and just before Nehemiah's second term as Persian commissioner; between 460 and 430 would be about right.

Zec 9:1–11:17. The first oracle

Christian interest may be roused by the prophecy of the king coming on the donkey and the popular interpretation of this as a sign of humility. It should be kept in mind that Solomon on his accession entered Jerusalem on the royal donkey of his father David (1 Kg 1:38) and that the beast was a sign of grandeur in Israelite society.

Those who are chagrined at their making such a mistake may be comforted by Matthew's mistaking Zechariah's poetic parallelism to mean that the messiah would ride on two animals (cf Mt 21:2).

The exodus imagery of the return of the exiles in chapter 9 is developed into the Joshua entry into the promised land (10:10f), but the main image of the first of the two oracle collections is that of the shepherd with which it ends.

The shepherd story of 11:4ff is almost a cultic play. The prophet is told to mime the part of a new shepherd (Yahweh himself) who will take over the flocks of the wicked shepherds. 11:6 is to be omitted as a late intrusion. Perhaps the prophet acted all this in the sheep-market. The old shepherds are dismissed one after another (there may be a reflection here of some jockeying for political and religious leadership in Jerusalem) and all seems set for a great and joyful grazing. But the sheep turn on the good shepherd and in frustration—and who can blame a man for any amount of fury when sheep turn on him?—he gives up his charge, breaking his crook. The old leaders come back and affect so to despise the lad sent by Yahweh that when he asks for his reward for his work he is told that he is worth only the price of a slave (cf Ex 31:32) and he, in anger at the outrage offered Yahweh, throws the silver down in the temple. This was an incident held in mind by those who put together the passion narratives (cf Mt 26:15 and 27:3ff).

A second shepherd play follows in which the prophet dresses as an incompetent shepherd (it is perhaps anachronistic to suggest that the shepherd's incompetence being discernible in his clothes puts this role well within the range of some Petit Trianon courtier) and simply chews the day away, caring not at all for the lost sheep. There follows a curse upon the false leaders.

Obviously the imagery of this oracle depends on the curse pronounced by Ezekiel against the false shepherd (Ez 34:1) and the promise that Yahweh will shepherd his own flock.

Zec 12:1–14:20. The second oracle

The day of Yahweh will come when Yahweh takes all sense and vigour from the neighbouring nations, and this oracle begins with a demonstration of Yahweh's rights over all creation.

12:10b ought to be translated 'they will look on me whom they have insulted'. Yahweh's deliverance of the people brings them to repent their previous insults and to join in public mourning ceremonies. This would give a sense roughly parallel with that of Ez 36:16ff where Yahweh tells the people that after their insults he will forgive them and bring them back to a happy rest in Jerusalem where 'you will loathe yourselves for your sins and your filthy practices' (Ez 36:31). The verb used there for 'profaning the name' of Yahweh can also mean 'pierce', and at Zec 12:10b 'piercing' is almost certainly a metaphor for 'insulting'.

The kind of ceremony to be performed shows that if the piercing is metaphorical, the metaphor has been forceful enough to suggest a taking-over of pagan cults connected with mourning for a stricken hero. The people will weep as for a dead prince, the first-born legal inheritor of the kingdom. Though in recent Israelite history Megiddo was famous as the place where the good king Josiah was assassinated, and though the Syrian version of this passage actually refers to Josiah in its gloss that Israel will mourn for 'the son of Amon', and though 2 Chron 35:25 makes it clear that a lament attributed to Jeremiah was still sung for Josiah, this mourning would have taken place in Jerusalem itself and not on the open plain among the fields. I think it more likely that the oracle here refers to the great mourning ritual for the dead fertility god of the Megiddo plain. The reference to Hadad, the storm-god of rains, and Rimmon, the god of Damascus, suggests that the rite was like that we know from surviving Ugaritic texts when the Canaanites prayed at the turn of the year for the fertilising of their crops, crying:

Puissant Baal is dead,
The Prince, the Lord of the Earth is perished.

Ez 8:14 suggests that such wailings were made in Jerusalem. The Mesopotamian fertility hero Tammuz had his weepers at the north gate of the temple. And it is obvious that the story of Jephthah's daughter (Jg 11:34ff) is a late explanation of such fertility weepings in Israel.

With this background in mind we can see that this oracle describes how the people of Jerusalem will go out in a mourning procession, each walking together as in the great procession of joy in Ps 68 until, at the moment of great repentance and weeping, the fountain of water for which they pray springs up.

At that moment everything shall be well in the land. The false prophets shall be disowned by their families, and those wounds they gave themselves in their ecstatic dances (cf 1 Kg 18:28) shall be covered up. These wounds were especially associated with the lament for the dead Baal. The Ugaritic text of the lament describes how the mourner puts on sackcloth and then 'gashes himself with a stone knife' cutting his cheeks, his chin, his arm, his chest, and even by some curious contortion in the ritual dance, his back, all the while crying 'Baal is dead! What shall become of the people?'

The oracle returns to the image of a fountain arising in Jerusalem at 14:8ff on the day when Israel's enemies will be routed by Yahweh and everyone in the world depend for their water upon this Jerusalem spring. Even Egypt, which might suppose its water-supply safe, will be reduced to dependence upon Israel's good-will, for if that nation fail to attend the feast of tabernacles its waters will turn again to blood.

Zec 14:20. On that day the horse-bells will become sacred like the bells on the high priest's vestment (cf Ex 28:35 and 36) and no longer sound a warning of the war-cavalry's approach, the cooking pots shall be made of gold, and everything shall become 'sacred to Yahweh'.

Mal 1:1–4:5. The third oracle

This oracle, which now constitutes our book of Malachi,

consists of a series of dramatic situations constructed
according to the following pattern:

  (i) Yahweh complains that the people do not serve him
properly;

 (ii) The people object that Yahweh is complaining
quite unjustifiably;

(iii) The justification of Yahweh's complaint is asserted,
either by Yahweh or by his representative the prophet.

1 Mal 1:1–5

Since prophecies are not made in a vacuum it would
seem that the people of Israel had been having such a
poor time that they had begun to question the fundamental concept of their faith. The prophet demon-
strates Yahweh's fidelity by pointing to Edom's troubles.
He must be referring to the raids by the Nabatean tribesmen on the rock towns of Edom. A significant post-
exilic claim for Yahweh's universal dominions occurs at
1:5.

2 Mal 1:6–2:9

Yahweh points to the offering of tainted animals that the
governor would not take as his due tribute (cf Lev 22:20
and Deut 15:21, 17:1). The insult is said to be offered
to the 'name' of Yahweh, and this evidences to the popular acceptance of the sophisticated distinction of the new
deuteronomist theology between Yahweh, who dwells in
his sky-home (Deut 26:15) and his 'name' which dwells
in the temple among men (Deut 12:5; 14:24).

Mal 1:10. Yahweh suggests that someone should shut
the doors of the temple and the farce of useless sacrifice

cease. Ironically, the sacrifices that are acceptable are being offered not in Jerusalem but in foreign parts. It is not clear whether these sacrifices are being offered by Jews of the diaspora or by foreigners in their cults. In either case the sacrifices are of praise and obedience offered by all, not of animals and cereals presented in the careful rites of the priestly caste. Perhaps the composer of this oracle, like Zerubbabel in his letter to the satraps (Ez 5:11) was prepared to take service of the Persian 'god of heaven' as service of Yahweh.

Mal 1:12. The complaint of Yahweh becomes a nag which goes over and over the same cause. And the attack on the cultic leaders continues in chapter 2.

The blessing pronounced by the priest was the most solemn moment of the temple ritual. When Yahweh says he will turn this blessing into a curse he is threatening a return to chaos which will be worse than the topsy-turvy universe envisaged by Joel. The liturgy has become meaningless for the priests and Yahweh threatens to render it meaningless for everyone else. He threatens to remove his name from the temple, for it was only at the moment of the blessing that the name was pronounced. The very distinction of Israel as Yahweh's folk is about to be taken away.

The rejection of the cult is symbolised in the paralysis of the arm that is stretched to the altar as if it were the arm of the apostate Jeroboam (1 Kg 13:5), and the flinging of dung upon the priestly vestments which had to be preserved from all defilement if the priest were to approach the altar. The dung includes that offal drawn from the beasts and thrown aside as totally unclean.

Mal 2:4. The 'covenant with Levi' refers to the levite

blessing of Moses (Deut 33:8ff) and we may take it that
the prophet was happy to accept the controversial identification of 'levite' and 'priest'.

Mal 2:7. The levitical priest is 'the messenger of Yahweh'. The same word, *mal'akhi*, is used at 3:1 for the
eschatological messenger of Yahweh whose function has
been transposed to a proper name for the author of the
oracle. There may be a suggestion here that the new era
will be announced by a levitical messenger.

3 **Mal 2:10-16**

The covenant included regulations forbidding marriage
with those who worshipped other gods (Ex 34:16;
Deut 7:3), and the assumption here seems to be that
those who married such women fell, like Solomon, under
the spell of their gods.

The marriages of covenant folk are indissoluble and
ordered towards the procreation and education of good
Hebrews. There is a literary patterning of some sophisti-
cation here, with the repetition of 'one' and 'spirit'. The
one Lord who created men (2:10), in marriage creates
one flesh (2:15a), and to this one flesh Yahweh has
given his spirit (2:15b) and the husband must therefore
be careful for this spirit (2:15c).

4 **Mal 2:17-3:5**

This section is designed as part of the Israelite discussion
of riches as signs of virtue being rewarded. The number of
counter-examples has grown so great that the bolder
spirits have been saying that Yahweh does not care
about virtue. The author of the oracle puts all blame on

men and suggests that they wait for the final coming for
making their final judgement.

The text suggests that after the arrival of the herald to
prepare the way, Yahweh will come to his temple 'and
the angel of the covenant'. Is this angel to be considered
a third comer? Yahweh himself is sometimes referred to
as an angel, at the meeting, for example, with Hagar on
the road to Shur (Gen 16:7), in Jacob's blessing of
Joseph's sons (Gen 48:16) and, most famously, at the
burning bush (Ex 3:2), so the identification is certainly
possible. But in Galatians (3:19) Paul, relying on his
knowledge of Jewish lore, speaks of the law being given
to Moses by an angelic intermediary. Malachi may be
referring here to this angel's return at the end of the covenant history.

When he comes, whether 'he' be the herald, the angel,
or Yahweh, he will be concerned with the purification of
the liturgy. He will cleanse those priests against whom
he has complained so that they may offer a pure sacrifice
at the centre of the Hebrew world (cf the reference
to the pure sacrifice at the fringes of that world,
1:11).

The images of purification are quite easily compre-
hended, the scouring of the golden vessels and the washing
of the be-dunged vestments would be quickly grasped as
signs of an inner purification.

The list of sinners against Yahweh's social order includes, like that of Ex 22:17, Lev 20:6, and Is 47:9, the
sorcerer who undermined the ordinary means of the
good life in Yahweh's order. The basic pattern of this list
seems to come from Ex 22:17–22, with its denunciations
of the sorcerers, the sexual offenders, the oppressors of
widows and orphans, and the men who exploit the ner-
vous foreigner.

5 Mal 3:6–12

The prophet's interest in the levitical priesthood leads
him to bring Yahweh's authority to bear on those who
duck their responsibility to pay the cultic tithe. The
reference at verse 9 is to the coming down of the curses of
Deut 27 and 28.

The floodgates of heaven are those which were opened
over the world at the time of Noah, and those who pray
for rain at the autumn festival evidently feel quite confi-
dent that Yahweh will remember his rainbow promise to
shut the floodgates when waters enough have poured
through.

Mal 3:12. The liturgical cry 'Blessed be God' (cf, for example, Ps 66:20; 68:35) is linked here with the blessing
given to Israel (cf Is 62:4 and the wedding rites of Yahweh and Israel his delight).

6 Mal 3:13–4:3

The prophet, again having recourse to eschatological
concepts to deal with present injustice, refers to Yahweh's record of men's actions. The doctrine of personal
immortality is not necessarily implied here, any more
than Egyptian notions of the sun-god with blessing hands,
or Persian notions of the god of light as a winged disc,
are necessarily supported by the prophet's reference to
the sun of righteousness.

The last verse seems to be a development of the references to the messenger of 2:7 and 3:1, identifying this
messenger with Elijah. The ascent of Elijah (2 Kg 2:11)
was not a death, and the prophet is canonising the popular notion that Elijah is still living in heaven and, again
without considering how this can be, is employing this

notion for eschatological purposes. The return of Elijah
as Yahweh's herald on the day became a common theme
of Jewish apocalyptic (cf Enoch 90:31) and found its
way into the new testament (Mt 11:14 etc).

1. What kind of 'sacrifice' do we think God wants from us?

*2. What do we think of Malachi's emphasis on the in-
dissolubility of the marriages of the faithful?*

*3. Does it seem important that the inspired author of the first
gospel misunderstood an idea in the earlier scriptural writings?*

Daniel

Bernard Robinson

Introduction

It seems to be the way with obscure things (such is human nature) that there are never wanting ingenious men to tell the world how transparently clear they are. To such men the Dark Lady of the Sonnets is all light, and the purpose of the pyramids self-evident. On no book of the bible, save perhaps the last, has their ingenuity produced so many clear but mutually contradictory interpretations as on the book of Daniel. The history of the exegesis of the book is strewn with the whited bones of those who thought they knew—knew that the little horn was their reigning king or pope, knew that the seventy weeks would end next Wednesday, knew that the kingdom of the saints was their own little sect. Their failure and disappointment must give us pause and make us ask whether it is profitable for a study group to give its attention to so cryptic a book: is there any reason why the exegetes of today should be able to see better than their predecessors, or why now at last we should suppose Daniel to have given up its secrets and to mock no longer the efforts of its interpreters?

I think there is. In the past men have assumed without question the nature, the literary *genre*, of the book, have taken it for what it itself claims to be, a book of prophecy dating from half a millennium before Christ, and

have blithely gone on to ask whether there are any signs
that the end foretold in the book is yet coming to pass.
The critical scholarship of today, on the other hand,
stops to consider the literary form of the book, and having done so produces an interpretation the main outline
of which finds general agreement among scholars: a
situation which contrasts strongly with that of previous
times, when conflicting interpretations succeeded each
other with amazing rapidity.

Though they differ considerably in their interpretation
of some individual texts, there is a general consensus of
opinion among scholars on the following points: (1)
That the book, in its present form at least, dates from the
second, and not—as ostensibly—from the sixth century
BC; (2) That the book belongs to the *genre* of apocalyptic
and not that of prophecy. The implications of these two
facts (as they may safely be called) is, as will be seen,
that attempts to find in Daniel allusion to world events
of one's own day are so much wasted effort.

When one calls Daniel apocalyptic and not prophecy,
one means that, though it purports to give prophecies
made by one Daniel in Babylon in the time of the exile,
it was really written much later, at a time when most of
the events 'prophesied' had already occurred. The unknown author of the book wrote in the time of the persecution of the Jews by the Seleucid king Antiochus IV
Epiphanes: he tells stories of how Babylonian kings who
persecuted Jews in the sixth century were thwarted
(thereby implying that Antiochus himself will be no
more successful in the long run) and then makes Daniel
give a brief account (a veiled account in which no names
are given) of the course of Jewish history between the
exile and the time of Antiochus (this in the form of prophecy): the culmination of the narrative is the death of

Antiochus, which had not yet occurred, so that this, as has been observed, is the only real prophecy in the book. The *raison d'être* of the book is the encouragement of the author's afflicted countrymen by showing them that God is in control of history and has protected and will protect his chosen people; the reason for the use of pseudonymity and of the seemingly disingenuous device of *post-eventum* prophecy is more a matter for controversy, and must be briefly discussed, though justice can scarcely be done to all the arguments in such a necessarily summary examination. Several views will be examined.

(1) Some claim that the author of Daniel was following a tradition already established in the ancient world (there is some evidence of the existence of such a tradition among the Greeks and the Egyptians). If it is true that the *genre* of pseudonymous apocalyptic was already established, it is not surprising that our author should find it very convenient for his purposes, for it gave him a way of safely sniping at the ruling powers by writing a book which ostensibly was a collection of old and obscure prophecies, but in fact was nothing less than a very acute and relevant tract for the times. To the cursory glance of Seleucid government agents it would appear harmless enough, whereas the Jewish readers for whom it was intended would not take long to recognise the book for what it truly was.

(2) A number of scholars say that the author wrote in the name of Daniel because he would thus stand a better chance of a hearing than if he wrote in his own name. Some even go so far as to say that he was keen on getting his book included in the canon of scripture and that his best hope of doing so was by pretending that it was the work of a sixth century prophet which had recently come

to light (actually, though the book got into the canon it was placed not among the prophets but in the third division of the OT, among the so-called 'writings'). It is implicit in such views that the writer set out to deceive not only the Seleucids but also his Jewish countrymen.

(3) H. H. Rowley has sought to explain the use of pseudonymity in terms of the genesis of the book. Daniel has come down to us partly in Hebrew and partly in Aramaic (Hebrew 1:1–2:4a; 8:1–end. Aramaic 2:4b–7:28), a fact for which a number of explanations have been put forward. Rowley believes that the stories which constitute Dan 2–6 were first issued one at a time, in Aramaic, and somewhat later chapter 7 was added, again in Aramaic; later on the author published the visions of Daniel (Dan 8–12), but this time in Hebrew for they were intended for a less popular audience. In Dan 2 the author had already made Daniel prophesy about the future up to the second century, and this idea he extended in 8–12, which he wrote in the first person in the name of Daniel (thus for the first time resorting to pseudonymity, for the Daniel stories of Dan 1–6 are not pseudonymous but anonymous): this device, thinks Rowley, was not adopted in order to deceive, but on the contrary in order to reveal the author's identity with the author of the earlier Daniel stories: it is, says Rowley, as if Dorothy Sayers after publishing her detective stories anonymously for some years had produced yet another, this time under the pseudonym 'Lord Peter Wimsey'. The final stage in the growth of the book came with the composition of chapter 1, in Hebrew, to stand as an introduction to the whole corpus.

(4) D. S. Russell believes that the author's intention was to express what he thought the sixth century Daniel *would* have said had he been alive in the second century.

Just as the rabbis felt that they belonged to an age-old tradition going back to Moses, 'the fountain-head of all lawgiving' and treated all legal formulations as Mosaic, so the apocalyptists attributed their own effusions to some ancient figure whose spiritual descendants they felt themselves to be. Russell supports his view with weighty arguments about Hebrew concepts of corporate personality, contemporaneity and the like, but two major difficulties remain even if one accepts the validity of these concepts:

(a) As Rowley says, as far as we know the sixth-century prophet Daniel is an invention of the second-century author of the book, and if this is so then Russell's view would seem to fall to the ground. True there is a sage called Dan'el mentioned at Ez 14:14, 20; 28:3, and in the 14/13th-century Ugaritic texts, but his name is spelt differently from our Daniel and he is clearly envisaged as living many centuries before the exile. (b) The parallel with the rabbis will not hold: the rabbis maintained that all law is *logically implicit* in the Pentateuch, and it is surely not credible that the apocalyptists believed that their messages could similarly be logically derived from the revelations of an Enoch, an Ezra or a Daniel.

If we are prepared to drop the supposed parallel with the rabbis and, despite the different spelling, identify the names Daniel and Dan'el, and also posit the existence of a tradition of a sixth-century Daniel prophesying in Babylon, a modified form of Russell's position may yet be salvaged, along these lines: Daniel of Babylon was thought of as a second Dan'el (just as, to take an example given by Russell himself, Ezra is in 2 Esdras 14 thought of as a second Moses); Daniel is, in other words, thought of as standing in the tradition of the ancient sage Dan'el.

In his turn the second-century apocalyptist thinks of himself as standing in the tradition of both of them and as being, as it were, an extension of their personality.

We will not presume to judge between these various views on the origin of pseudonymity. Suffice it to say that the other books that were written in imitation of Daniel (for Daniel was the first of a whole series of pseudonymous apocalypses: 1 Enoch, 2 Esdras, 2 Baruch, *The Testament of the Twelve Patriarchs*, Revelation, and others) took over the use of pseudonymity from Daniel. They share too with their parent book a taste for the exotic, the esoteric, the bizarre and the symbolic: they love, for instance, to juggle with numbers and to represent individuals and empires under the form of beasts or reptiles. They are also bookish in outlook: the word of God is not something to be spoken out boldly, as it was to the prophets: it has to be written down in a book and hidden away for centuries and then read and understood only by the wise. Again, apocalyptists share a common view of history: the past falls easily into neat divisions, empires rise and fall according to a set determination by God ('the most high ruleth in the kingdom of men', Dan 4:25), and the culmination of all history, when the kingdoms of the world will rise with monstrous violence against God's elect, is just around the corner (in the apocalypses, it should be noted, the gentile nations are not the tools of God, as they were to an Isaiah or a Jeremiah, but always the adversaries of God); an apocalypse is always conceived as a message of comfort written to encourage men on the eve of Armageddon: lift up your heads, the apocalyptist says, for God will shortly rout his enemies and the saints of God will triumph.

Since the apocalyptists usually expected an early end, which did not happen, one might be forgiven for thinking that, as discredited prophets, they have no serious claims on our attention. Yet two of the apocalypses (the original one, Daniel, and Revelation) are included within the canon of scripture and must therefore carry for the christian a perennial divine message. I take this permanent message to be this—that God is the lord of history, shaping and directing it according to the mystery of his will: in good time he will emerge triumphant, vindicating the sufferings of his holy ones. I also find permanently salutary the doctrine of the apocalyptists that evil resides not only in individuals but in corporate structures too, such as governments. So long as we think of sin as a matter only of the guilt of individuals, we have not plumbed the depth of biblical teaching about evil (expressed in the NT in a variety of forms, for instance 'Satan' and, in Paul, 'the body of sin' and 'the principalities and powers'). A man is either helped or impeded in his conduct by the structures of the communities of which he is a member, and evil structures, evil laws, evil customs have a pervasive effect by which none but a few elect souls can help being contaminated. The pity of it is that most regimes have a bland, conditioning effect which ensures that few of their subjects are aware of the extent to which their whole being is influenced by the system. Each political set-up, in so far as it falls short of the ideal (and which does not?) is a rebirth of the monster which the author of Daniel saw rising from the great sea (which was a mythological way of talking of forces which disrupt the beneficent will of the creator to impart unity and harmony to his world), each government is, in the language of the book of Revelation, 'Babylon the great, the mother of harlots'. It is easy enough to recognise the scarlet women in totalitarian regimes, but in a lesser degree the christian should, I would suggest, see her (and, seeing her,

denounce her) in every system. This is not to say that one
should be negative in one's attitude to political matters—
the 'kingdom of the saints of the most high' whose realisa-
tion we await is certainly not without its political side—
but the future kingdom can never come if we are content
with substitutes which degrade men, inhibit personal
responsibility and, in varying degrees, undermine human
morality. We need, perhaps, to add to the prophetic
vision that kings and empires can be the tools of God the
apocalyptic conviction that they can be, and perhaps
always in some sort are, tools in the hand of 'the man of
sin'.

A brief account must now be given of life in Palestine
in the second century, for without an outline knowledge
of the history of the period, all the oblique but important
historical allusions in the book of Daniel must be lost on
the reader.

In the mid-fourth century BC the Persian empire,
which included Palestine, fell into the hands of Alexander
the Great of Macedon. On the death of that great empire-
builder, his dominions were fought over acrimoniously
by would-be successors: from sometime before 301 till
198 BC Judah was under the sway of the Ptolemies, the
rulers of Egypt, and all the evidence suggests that the
Jews found them tolerant and lenient overlords; in 198
the Seleucid king Antiochus III (Antiochus the Great,
223–187) took over the possessions of the Ptolemies, including Palestine. Such evidence as we possess (it is scanty
enough) suggests that at first the Seleucids were as easy-
going with the Jews (granting them tax remittances, and
supporting their temple worship) as had been the
Ptolemies before them. Towards the end of his reign,
however, Antiochus III found himself much harassed by
the Romans, and lack of money induced him to initiate a

policy widely followed by his successors, Seleucus IV (187–175) and Antiochus IV Epiphanes (175–163), of looting temples: Antiochus III himself died looting a temple in Elam, Seleucus tried to plunder the Jewish temple (2 Mac 3:4–40; cf Dan 11:20), and Antiochus IV laid sacrilegious hands on temples in Rome, Egypt, Parthia and Jerusalem.

From the time of Antiochus III Greek culture grew in influence in Palestine, and there were Greek colonies at Samaria (Sebaste), 'Ammân (Philadelphia), Acre (Ptolemais), Bethshan (Scythopolis) and Philoteria; it was Antiochus IV, however, who departed from precedent by attempting forcibly to impose Greek culture and religion on the Jews. He found his dominions in a parlous state, hard pressed on all sides, by Rome, Parthia and Egypt, and he looked to a policy of enforced hellenization as his best hope of uniting an unstable empire. Unfortunately for him, a policy which was not unsuccessful elsewhere proved useless against the stubborn and incomprehensible Jews.

At the time of the accession of Antiochus IV, the Jerusalem high-priesthood (the most important office among the Jews of this period) was held by an orthodox anti-hellenist, Onias III. Shortly after his succession Antiochus, in return for a gift of money (which was always in short supply with him) appointed Onias' brother Jason as high priest, deposing Onias himself. Jason showed himself very amenable to Antiochus' policies and abolished circumcision and introduced gymnasia into Palestine (it should be noted, lest this be thought an innocent enough innovation, that Greek sports were inseparable from Greek religious practices, and Jason was therefore covertly introducing pagan cults). In 172 a Jew called Menelaus outbid Jason for the high-priesthood, murdered Onias when the latter protested, and plundered the temple treasury. In 169 Jason, hearing a rumour of Antiochus' death, returned to Jerusalem and ousted Menelaus. Antiochus then intervened, reinstating Menelaus, and sending to Jerusalem (in 167) one Apollonius, who slaughtered many of the city's inhabitants and constructed a citadel (the 'Acra') on the hill opposite the temple. Finding that the intractableness of the Jews was based on their religion, which they refused to see subsumed into the syncretistic religious system which he was seeking to impose, Antiochus proceeded to proscribe the Jewish religion—at any rate, in its pure form: he abolished the sacrificial system and the observation of the sabbath and the festivals, forbade circumcision and ordered the burning of copies of the scriptures. Pagan altars were erected everywhere, and the Jews were forced to eat pork under pain of death. An altar to, and probably a statue of, Olympian Zeus was erected in the temple at Jerusalem: this marked the most daring of Antiochus' attempts to synthesise Yahwism with hellenism. It seems unlikely that Antiochus meant Zeus actually to replace Yahweh—rather, the two were to be identified: according to Josephus, the Samaritans had actually asked that their temple should be rededicated to Zeus, and the stubborn resistance of the Jews to the erection of what Daniel calls the abomination of desolation must have surprised as much as angered Antiochus. No course was left to him but open persecution: mothers who circumcised their sons were executed, men were put to death for refusing to eat unclean foods, and the observance of the sabbath became a capital offence. It was against this backcloth of terror that Daniel was written, a pamphlet intended perhaps for circulation in small study groups, so to say, of Hasidim (that is, orthodox Jews who

opposed hellenization): if this is so, this may offer an easy
explanation of how the author could have ensured that
his use of pseudonymity should not deceive his Jewish
readers, for he had only to explain the device by word of
mouth to his fellow Hasidim. However that may be, it
was at this critical time that Daniel was written, a message of hope for loyal, orthodox, persecuted Jews and a
promise of the destruction at the hand of God of their
cruel oppressors. The Maccabees who organised armed
rebellion against the Seleucid regime shortly afterwards
were probably much influenced by Daniel, and the independent Jewish state of sorts which emerged in 164
(inaugurated by the *Hanukkah* or rededication of the
temple after its defilement by Antiochus) if it did not
completely fulfil the author of Daniel's hope, owed much
to the inspiration of his book.

When, throughout this outline, I speak of the 'author'
of Daniel, I refer to the Maccabean-period writer who
put the books together in the form (less, perhaps, a few
short scribal additions) in which it now stands in the
Hebrew bible. It seems by no means impossible, however,
that in Dan 1–6 this writer was using sources, perhaps
oral but more probably written, which had originated
much earlier. The presence of some Persian words in the
Daniel stories naturally suggests that they had a literary
prehistory. Ginsberg, then, may well be correct in supposing that the raw material of Dan 1–6 was originally
composed about 300 BC with, of course, a very different
situation in mind than the Maccabean one. It is also
possible that these stories contain, in a much altered
form, some authentic memories from Babylonian times,
for it has plausibly been argued that the tales of the
dream, statue and madness of Nebuchadrezzar derive
from true accounts of another, less well-known

Babylonian king, Nabonidus, who fled from his court for seven, or perhaps ten, years after having antagonised the priests of Marduk, who resented his repairing the temple and statue of the moon deity Sin (we also have texts alluding to Nabonidus' reliance on oneiromancers). Such stories may have been brought to Palestine, as McNamara holds, by Jews returning to their homeland from Babylonia in the second century BC. However, the historicity of these stories, and the reason for their originally having been composed (if they were) in c 300 BC are considerations of a secondary nature: it may well be that some genuine recollections about Nabonidus are embedded in Dan 1–6, it may also quite possibly be the case that the stories in this first half of the book were originally written up in less troubled times than the Maccabean period, in times when the Jews lived peaceably under foreign rule and rose to high position at court, and that the intention of the Jew who first gave these stories written form was not to afford his readers a lesson in endurance, but to encourage them to commend themselves by prudent means to their overlords; yet we owe the preservation of these stories to the second century writer who took them over, touched them up and turned them, most cleverly, into comments on the events of his own day. It is the message of this writer that I shall be considering in this outline, a message which comes through, I think, loud and clear, and which speaks to our condition, whereas the message of the author(s) of the 'originals' is conjectural, as indeed is his (their) very existence.

Note The Greek additions to Daniel (*Susannah, Bel and the Dragon*, etc) will not be discussed in this commentary.

Book list

J. Barr, 'Daniel' in *Peake's Commentary* (new edition, 1962).

S. R. Driver, *The Book of Daniel* (Cambridge Bible for Schools and Colleges) Cambridge, 1900.

H. L. Ginsberg, 'The composition of the Book of Daniel', *Vetus Testamentum* 4 (1954), pp 246–75.

H. L. Ginsberg, *Studies in Daniel* (*Texts and Studies of the Jewish Theological Seminary of America* XIV) 1948.

L. F. Hartman, 'Daniel' in *The Jerome Bible Commentary*, London, 1968.

E. W. Heaton, *The Book of Daniel* (Torch Bible) London, 1956.

M. D. Hooker, 'The "One like a son of man" in Daniel 7', ch 2 of *The Son of Man in Mark*, London, 1967.

M. McNamara, 'Daniel' in *The New Catholic Commentary on Holy Scripture*, London, 1969.

M. Noth, 'History in Old Testament apocalyptic', ch 7 of *The Laws in the Pentateuch and other essays*, Edinburgh etc, 1966.

N. W. Porteous, *Daniel, a commentary* (Old Testament Library), London, 1965.

H. H. Rowley, *The relevance of apocalyptic* (3rd ed) London, 1963.

H. H. Rowley, 'The unity of the Book of Daniel', ch 7 of *The Servant of the Lord and other essays* (2nd ed) London, 1952.

D. S. Russell, *The Method and Message of Jewish apocalyptic* (Old Testament Library) London, 1964.

K. Koch, *The Rediscovery of Apocalyptic* (Studies in Biblical Theology) London, 1972.

1
The Daniel stories
Dan 1:1–6:28

Dan 1:1–21. The dietary question

'In the third year of the reign of Jehoiakim king of Judah, Nebuchadrezzar king of Babylon came to Jerusalem and besieged it.' It is doubtful whether this is historical. In 604 (after Jehoiakim, who came to the throne in 609, had reigned for five years) Nebuchadrezzar (who succeeded his father Nabopolassar in August 605, and was thus not even king in Jehoiakim's third year) was in the Palestine area and captured and deported some of the population of the Philistine city of Ashkelon. It seems unlikely that he actually invaded Judah and besieged Jerusalem (2 Chron 36:6–7 does report such an invasion but the more historically reliable 2 Kings knows nothing of it). Probably our author has misunderstood 2 Kg 24:1, which tells how, when Nebuchadrezzar 'came up' (ie to Philistia in 604?) Jehoiakim became his vassal for three years, after which he rebelled: after a time (actually in 598/7) the Babylonians invaded Judah, and Jehoiachin, who in the meantime had succeeded his father Jehoiakim, was taken as an exile to Babylon.

This, the first of the Daniel stories, tells how Daniel and his companions were groomed for service in the royal court of Babylon, how they boldly refused to eat unclean meat and were allowed, experimentally, to take to a vegetarian diet, which proved so nutritious that all the rest of the young men at court were put on it.

Clearly the story is not intended to be read as propaganda for vegetarianism (though there is a school of thought in old testament times, represented by the Pentateuchal source 'P', which allows meat-eating only as a concession to the fall and degradation of man: Gen 1:29; 9:3): the moral of the story is obviously connected with the events of the author's own day. I think it likely that it was written before Antiochus' persecuting policy got seriously under way, at a time when, though there was already some pressure being put upon the Jews to conform, there was still hope that by making a firm stand one could win through without mishap, as Daniel is represented as doing: 2 Mac 5:27 tells how, before the Epiphanian persecution reached its height, Judas Maccabeus and his companions lived on wild herbs to avoid ritual pollution, just as the Daniel of the present story did.

The statement that Daniel 'continued until the first year of king Cyrus' (1:21; according to 10:1 he was actually still alive in Cyrus' third year) probably means that as a reward for his religious fidelity Daniel survived to see the edict of liberation which was promulgated in that year (Ezr 1:1): those who follow Daniel's example —such is the implication—will similarly live to see Jewish emancipation from the Seleucid yoke.

In the light of the terrible fate of those who did make the stand here advocated, this chapter with its tone of optimistic encouragement makes poignant reading. It is significant that within a short time the author had seen enough brave men brutally put to death for their religion to come to the conclusion that the vindication of the righteous must lie on the other side of the grave: he could

not believe that the Maccabean martyrs would not find
their reward, nor that their oppressors would escape
punishment, and therefore he departed from traditional
Jewish opinions by proclaiming a doctrine of resurrection from the dead (Dan 12).

Note the emphasis in this chapter, and in later ones
too, on *wisdom*: 'youths without blemish . . . skilful in all
wisdom . . . God gave them learning and skill in all
letters and wisdom . . . and in every matter of wisdom
and understanding concerning which the king enquired
of them, he found them ten times better than all the
magicians and enchanters that were in his kingdom.'
Heaton has pointed out that the figure of Daniel em-
bodies just about all the qualities and traits ascribed to a
wise man in the book of Ecclesiasticus, written some
fifteen years before Daniel:

> He researches into the wisdom of all the ancients,
>   he occupies his time with the prophecies . . .
>   he is at home with the niceties of parables . . .
> He enters the service of princes,
>   he is seen in the presence of rulers.
> He travels in foreign countries,
>   he has experienced human good and human evil
>
> (Sir 39)

It is hardly fanciful to see this portrayal of Daniel and his
companions as great sages as a deliberate bid by our
author to beat the Greeks of his own day at their own
game by showing Hebrew wisdom (*ḥokmah*), which is
essentially reliant on God, as more than a match for the
self-sufficient *sophia* on which the Greeks prided themselves so much.

*Commenting on the fate of those who died rather than break
the Jewish dietary laws, Porteous says: 'When we read the*

history of the past, we may have the feeling that the battles were
fought on the wrong ground and for the wrong issues. At the
same time it may well be better in the end that certain battles
should have been fought than that there was no issue worth
fighting for'. Do you agree?

Dan 2:1–49. Of dreams

Nebuchadrezzar has a dream which troubles him, and he
commands all his wise men to tell him the content and
the meaning of it, which all except Daniel are unable to
do. Daniel reveals that the dream concerned a great
statue which was part gold, part silver, part bronze and
part a mixture of iron and clay, and a great stone which
struck and broke the statue in pieces and then grew in
size till it filled the whole world. Nebuchadrezzar, says
Daniel, is the head of gold, and the other materials represent other kingdoms that will succeed his, until finally the
God of heaven will himself establish a kingdom (represented by the stone) which will last for ever.

The four kingdoms are doubtless Babylon, Media,
Persia and Greece (the last is represented as a mixture of
clay and iron with reference to the division of the empire
after the death of Alexander the Great between the
Ptolemaic and Seleucid houses, the latter of which finally
prevailed and is no doubt thought of as the iron element
in the kingdom). The kingdom established by God is the
independent Jewish state which the author of Daniel and
his contemporaries hoped to see; a hope which was partly
substantiated by the erection of the régime of the Has-
monean priest-kings, a régime, however, which left much
to be desired and persisted for only one century out of
the eternity here promised to it.

This chapter sits very loose to historical possibilities.
The imagination boggles at the idea of a pious Jew being

able to accept (even if it were offered to him) the position of leader of the astrologers and magicians of Babylon. Also, the idea, here only implicit but stated clearly enough later with the mention of 'Darius the Mede', that between the times of Babylonian and of Persian rule Babylon was in the hands of the Medes is quite false: the Babylonian and the Median empires were really concurrent. The idea of the four empires is probably not original: the Romans commonly spoke of four empires which had preceded their own—Assyria, Media, Persia, Macedonia—and the idea is thought quite probably to be of oriental origin. With this motif of the four empires Daniel combines the notion, a commonplace of ancient thinking (found in Persia and in Hesiod) of four world epochs characterised by gold, silver, bronze and iron, though the implication of progressive deterioration which the idea originally carried is largely ignored by our author, doubtless because there was no pattern of decline discernible in the four kingdoms of which he was writing.

The message of this chapter is simple enough, a message of comfort to the author's contemporaries who would shortly see the Seleucid régime swept away before the advent of a kingdom established by the God of heaven who alone 'changes times and seasons, removes kings and sets up kings, gives wisdom to the wise and knowledge to those who have understanding' (2:20–21).

Is it profitable to look for the meaning of history?

Dan 3:1–30. Ordeal by fire

The three companions of Daniel (who does not himself appear in this chapter: perhaps we have here an adaptation of a story which had originally no connection with Daniel) are put into a furnace for refusing to worship a golden image erected by Nebuchadrezzar: they emerge unscathed, and the Babylonians marvel at a God who is able to work such miracles for his devotees.

Golden statues were common in Babylonia, and casting people into the flames may well have been a favourite Babylonian form of execution (cf Jer 29:22), but despite these attempts at artistic verisimilitude it is clear that Nebuchadrezzar really stands in place of Antiochus IV in the story. We know from Herodotus (1:183) that Antiochus erected a golden statue, and it is surely significant that one of the instruments played by the court musicians (3:5 etc) is called a *symphonia* (a Greek loan word transliterated into Aramaic), an instrument— some sort of bagpipe—which is first mentioned in the second century as a favourite instrument of Antiochus IV: Polybius (26:10; 31:4) tells us that Antiochus chose low drinking companions and embarrassed the company by dancing to the sound of the *symphonia*.

The great point of the chapter lies in the words addressed by the three young men to the king: 'O Nebuchadrezzar, we have no need to answer you in this matter. If it be so, our God whom we serve is able to deliver us from the burning fiery furnace; and he will deliver us out of your hand, O king. But if not, be it known to you, O king, that we will not serve your gods or worship the golden image which you have set up' (3:17–18). In these bold, defiant sentences we catch the genuine accents of our author's attitude to the Seleucid oppressor, the attitude of one who hopes that God will intervene to strike down the persecutor, but even if he does not he will be faithful to his religious principles and face death rather than succumb.

Are there, perhaps, in the world today more subtle forms of idolatry and of conformity to the unjust demands of officialdom which are as dangerous as the more open form of infidelity envisaged here? Examples?

Dan 4:1-37. Nebuchadrezzar mad

This chapter begins in the first person as an epistle, a sort of court circular, from Nebuchadrezzar, lapses from verses 19 to 33 into the third, but ends as it had begun in the first. It recounts a vision which Daniel interprets as meaning that unless he repents (4:27) Nebuchadrezzar will go mad for seven 'times' (a grecism, meaning 'years') and live the life of a wild beast. This comes to pass, and at the end of the seven years Nebuchadrezzar, now restored to his wits, praises the God of heaven whose hand none can stay (4:35).

That Nebuchadrezzar ever had such a disagreeable experience there is no evidence, but the *Prayer of Nabonidus* from Qumran reflects a similar tradition about king Nabonidus, who retired to Teiman for seven years afflicted with some sort of ulcer, and after praying in vain to 'the gods of silver and gold . . . wood and stone and clay' was healed by a Jewish 'exorcist', on whose instructions he wrote a letter describing his experiences. Our story here about Nebuchadrezzar would appear to be a variant of the same tradition. It is obviously directed against Antiochus Epiphanes, who was nicknamed also 'Epimanes' (the mad): it carries the grim warning that unless Antiochus breaks off sinning, practises righteousness and shows mercy to the oppressed he will quite literally become the Epimanes that his enemies call him.

Is the notion of retributive punishment, which bulks so large in Daniel, repugnant to christian values?

Dan 5:1–30. A dinner party at the palace

This is a story of divine retribution for sacrilege: for drinking from the Jewish sacred vessels, stolen from the temple, and for invoking pagan gods, king Belshazzar, son of Nebuchadrezzar, loses his kingdom overnight as foretold in the cryptic writing on the wall, interpreted by Daniel. The kingdom then passes into the hands of Darius the Mede.

The story contains a number of historical 'howlers':

(1) Belshazzar was not the son of Nebuchadrezzar, but of Nabonidus (who was a *novus homo*).
(2) Belshazzar was never actually king, though as crown prince he administered the kingdom during his father's seven-year absence at Teiman.
(3) Babylon fell without violence according to inscriptions, and to the Persians not to the Medes (though Is 13:17ff; 21:1–10, which may have influenced Daniel, had foretold conquest by the Medes).
(4) The Medes never had a king called Darius.

The precise point of the writing on the wall is in doubt (indeed, the text itself is not certain), but it is probable that what Belshazzar is said to have seen is the names of three coins of decreasing value—the mina, the shekel and the paras or half-mina, and the primary, though implicit point of the inscription is perhaps to indicate the declining significance of either various world empires (Babylonians, Medes and Persians?) or of successive Babylonian kings (Nebuchadrezzar, Nabonidus, Belshazzar?). In his interpretation as given in the text, however, Daniel plays upon the names of these three coins: *mina* suggests the verb *manah*, to measure, *tekel* the verb *shakal*, to weigh, and *paras* the verb *paras* to divide (it also suggests the name 'Persia').

As we have seen in the introduction above, Antiochus
IV, like his father and his elder brother, was a great
plunderer of temples, and thus the story is intended to
warn Antiochus that his action in removing the sacred
vessels from the Jewish temple could lose him his life and
his kingdom.

*What limitations of theological outlook are revealed in this
chapter?*

Dan 6:1–28. The lions' den

The last of the Daniel stories tells how the satraps and
presidents of the provinces conspire against Daniel and
persuade the king to punish anyone who prays to or
worships any god or man except the king. For praying to
his God, Daniel is thrown to the lions, but takes no harm,
a fact which induces Darius to establish toleration of the
Jewish religion and to feed Daniel's enemies to the lions
in his place. The story is simple and straightforward: it is
meant to encourage the Jews to resist the paganism enforced by Antiochus and to frighten would-be informers
from betraying the orthodox into the hands of the government. It should be noted that the statue of Zeus set up by
Antiochus probably bore the king's own features (since
he claimed to be a divine incarnation) so that when the
story speaks of worshipping the king it is probably alluding to the cult of the statue put up by Antiochus.

*1. The satraps and the presidents are the culprits of this
story. What is their motivation?*
2. Does wickedness never pay?

2

The Daniel visions
Dan 7:1–12:13

Dan 7:1–28. The vision of the beasts and the son of man

Daniel dreams of four wild beasts which come out of the 'great sea'. Then he sees God sitting in a court of judgement, and 'one like a son of man' comes before him with the clouds of heaven and is given the rule of an everlasting kingdom. God explains that the beasts are four great kings who will rule on earth until such time as the kingdom is given to 'the saints of the most high'.

In the interpretation of the vision given in Dan 7 itself, the beasts represent kings, who themselves represent the empires over which they rule, and the son of man figure seems to represent 'the saints of the most high' or 'the people of the saints of the most high'. In other words the 'son of man' in Daniel is not an individual, and certainly not an individual messiah (as Rowley says, 'there is no evidence that the Son of Man was identified with the Messiah until the time of Jesus'). The beasts and the man-like figure all represent kingdoms, the beasts savage and brutish kingdoms, the man a wise and humane one. The author's meaning is that after the kingdoms of Babylon, Media, Persia and Macedon (the last beast is the worst, and its little horn with 'eyes like human eyes, and a mouth that was full of boasts' is clearly Antiochus iv: with Dan 7:25 cf 1 Mac 1:41ff) there will follow an everlasting kingdom of the holy people of Israel.

The above interpretation is not the only possible one, but it seems to me the most likely as well as the simplest. It should, however, be mentioned that in the *Similitudes of Enoch* (= 1 Enoch 37–71), a book written not long after Daniel (some even say before) there also occurs a 'son of man', who is clearly a supernatural figure, probably conceived of as both individual and collective; he was chosen 'before the creation of the world and for evermore' (48:6) to stand at the head of the heavenly company of righteous men who will one day inherit the kingdom, and he is set on God's throne to share the divine glory (51:3; 61:8) and to judge men and angels. At present he is hidden, but will in good time be revealed. Now, some have argued that the son of man in Daniel is also thought of as a supernatural or heavenly being: he comes with the clouds of heaven, which according to old testament usage is suggestive of a theophany, and also angelic beings are often represented in human form in the bible (eg in Daniel itself at 10:5). Further, in the phrase '(the people of) the saints of the most high' the saints may, if Noth and Dequeker are right, be not the people of Israel but the angels of God. Thus it is possible to argue that Dan 7 is foretelling the advent of a kingdom of the angels—perhaps in the sense that the men of the kingdom will be governed and directed by heavenly powers.

The dominion allowed to the 'little horn' (= Antiochus) is to last for three and a half years ('a time, times and half a time'): whether this was meant as a vague indication of a very short time, or as an exact period, is not clear. At any rate, it was not far out: the persecution of the Jews by Antiochus began in 168/7 and finished, with the rededication of the temple, in 164.

M. D. Hooker says: 'The pattern of the vision in Dan 7 has been shaped by the primitive myth of creation; the emergence of the beasts from the sea, their defeat by Yahweh, and the bestowal of dominion on a human figure, are all motifs taken from this background.' Not all would agree with this, but the use of the expression 'the great sea'— almost a technical term for the primeval sea of mythology—and also the reference in 7:2 to the 'four winds' which have no real function to perform here, though they have point in the Babylonian creation story, would seem to be quite strong evidence. The myth of the primeval struggle between God and the chaos-dragon (Tiamat/Rahab/Leviathan) is vestigially present in several texts of the old testament (eg Gen 1; Ps 74:12–17; 89:10ff; Job 7:12ff) and there is no need to posit direct dependence of Dan 7 on Babylonian sources. The point in using the creation motif is perhaps, as Heaton says, to indicate that 'the nations were setting themselves in opposition to the Rule of God and were in fact, undoing the work of creation and reducing the world to chaos'.

Are there both political and theological lessons in the 'son of man' passage?

Dan 8:1–27. The ram and the he-goat

From this point to the end of the book is in Hebrew (1:1–2:4 is also in Hebrew, the rest of the book is in Aramaic).

Under the likeness of a ram and a he-goat, the rise of the kingdoms of Media-Persia and of Alexander is here recounted. The horns sprouted by the he-goat represent the different fragments into which Alexander's empire resolved itself after his death—the little horn again represents Antiochus ('a king of bold countenance, one who understands riddles': = a master of intrigue—so Porteous). He, Antiochus, is again allowed a reign of $3\frac{1}{2}$ years, after which he is to die 'broken by no human hand'. According to 2 Mac 9, Antiochus died in Persia of a loathsome disease, so the prophecy here is more accurate than that of 11:40 and 45, which makes Antiochus die apparently in battle and on the soil of Palestine.

Dan 9:1–27. The seventy weeks

Jer 25:11ff and 29:10 posit a period of seventy years for Babylon's dominion over the Jews. Probably this period was intended by the prophet as a round figure, but in any case he was not far out, for the rebuilding of the temple was finished in 516, just about seventy years after the fall of the city. Perhaps because the return and the restoration had in fact been something less of a triumph than Jeremiah had seemed to anticipate, and had not led to Jewish independence, the author of Daniel here sets himself to produce an ingenious reinterpretation of Jeremiah's prophecy. In doing this he is following an already established tradition whereby unfulfilled or only partly fulfilled prophecies can be recast later in a different mould and be made to bear a meaning other than they originally carried (Ezekiel takes Jeremiah's apparently unfulfilled prophecies of the coming of a foe from the north—eg Jer 1:14; 3:1–6:30—and gives them, in his prophecy of 'Gog from the land of Magog', Ez 38:1, an eschatological function. In this he is followed by Deutero-Zechariah, Zech 14:2, and Joel, Jl 2:20.) Thus by making the seventy years into seventy weeks of years (ie

70 × 7 years) Daniel makes Jeremiah prophesy the death of Antiochus IV. For details of how this works out, see other commentaries.

Dan 10:1–12:13. Some history

These last three chapters make up the last vision of Daniel, in which he sees no cryptic animals this time, but is given by a heavenly being a straightforward survey of Seleucid history in some detail, leading up to the death of Antiochus (which itself is not described in such detail, as it had not occurred at the time of writing). After the death of Antiochus, the Maccabean martyrs will rise from their graves to glory (12:2), and their oppressors and the apostate dead, whose sins cry out for punishment, will rise to 'shame and everlasting contempt'.

The 'mighty king' of 11:3 is Alexander, the expressions 'king of the north' and 'king of the south' indicate the Seleucid and Ptolemaic kings respectively, and the particular 'king of the north' spoken of from 11:21 onwards is Antiochus Epiphanes. The death foretold for him (11:45) is, as we have said, inaccurate, but the reason why our text makes him die in Palestine is interesting: it is probable that Daniel is again reinterpreting prophecy—the words that Ezekiel makes God address to Gog (themselves a reinterpretation of some words of Jeremiah: see above): 'I will lead you against the mountains of Israel . . . You shall fall upon the mountains of Israel . . . You shall fall in the open field,' Ez 39:2–5). Thus Antiochus is interpreted as being Ezekiel's Gog, who is himself a reinterpretation of Jeremiah's foe from the north.

Interesting also is 12:12. The previous verse foretells Jewish liberation after 1290 days. There follows the verse: 'Blessed is he who waits and comes to the 1335 days.' Probably we have here yet another case of re-interpretation: this time by a reader of the book some $3\frac{1}{2}$ years after it was written—the deliverance had not come though the 1290 days had passed, so he discreetly and hopefully took up his pen and extended the period by a couple of months! The period of 1290 days is itself an extension of the 1150 days of 8:14, but probably in this case the extending was done by the author himself.

'Many shall run to and fro, and knowledge shall in-crease,' 12:4. Amos had described people wandering to and fro in search of knowledge without finding it (Am 8:12): Daniel is able to promise that their search will no longer be in vain (if indeed the Hebrew text pre-serves the correct reading: the Greek has the reading 'wickedness' instead of 'knowledge').

1. How does the viewpoint of Daniel differ from that of OT *prophetical books?*

2. Is the apocalyptist's view of the world as a battleground between the righteous on the one side and, on the other, evil in-carnated in a person or a political institution, valid?

3. Michael Goulder has written to the effect that the Revela-tion of John cannot be relevant to our generation until we begin to witness to Christ by recognising in our western civilisation 'the whore of Babylon for our time'—'we need to see God's wrath with our iniquitous society, and it is our lack of persecutors, due to our failure of witness, which makes the book irrelevant'. Is Daniel perhaps inaccessible to us for the same reason—through our fault, not the book's?